The Gustave A. and Mamie W. Efroymson
Memorial Lectures
Delivered March 1995 at the
Hebrew Union College-Jewish Institute of Religion
Cincinnati, Ohio

Ruth Kartun-Blum

with drawings by Menashe Kadishman

Profane
Scriptures

Reflections on the Dialogue
with the Bible
in Modern Hebrew Poetry

Hebrew Union College Press
Cincinnati

Permission to reprint "The Real Hero of the Sacrifice" by Yehuda Amichai
from *Yehuda Amichai: A Life of Poetry 1948-1994* (1994) granted by
HarperCollins Publishers, Inc.
Permission to reprint T. Carmi's translations of "Isaac" by Amir Gilboa,
"Heritage" by Haim Gouri, and "A Moment" by Nathan Zach in *The Penguin
Book of Hebrew Verse* (1981) granted by Penguin UK.
Permission to reprint Harold Schimmel's translation of "The Poem on the
Africs" by Avot Yeshurun from *The Syrian-African Rift and Other Poems* (1980)
granted by the Jewish Publication Society.

Library of Congress Cataloging-in-Publication Data
Kartun-Blum, Ruth.
Profane Scriptures : reflections on the dialogue with the
Bible in modern Hebrew poetry / Ruth Kartun-Blum : with drawings by
Menashe Kadishman.
p. cm.
Includes bibliographical references.
ISBN 0-87820-054-1
1. Israeli poetry–History and criticism. 2. Bible. O.T.—In literature.
3. Isaac (Biblical patriarch) in literature. 4. Wallach, Yona–
Criticism and interpretation. I. Kadishman, Menashe, 1932-. II. Title.
PJ5024.K26 1999
892.4'10938221-DC21   99-10451
                                                       CIP

Cover design by Menashe Kadishman and Bilha Kadishman
Copyright © 1999 by the Hebrew Union College Press
Hebrew Union College-Jewish Insittute of Religion
Printed on acid free paper in the United States of America
Typeset by Posner and Sons Ltd. Jerusalem, Israel
Distributed by Wayne State University Press
4809 Woodward Avenue, Detroit, MI 48201

For Amos, Hilit, and Gabriella

Contents

Preface

This book is about twentieth-century Hebrew poetry rereading its Scriptures, about sons battling with distant fathers and close fathers, and about daughters trying to find their place. In poetic and political terms, a filial struggle for identity means a struggle over the possession of language and the crucial right to interpret the present moment in new terms—a difficult struggle indeed in a language that seems to be hypnotized by its past.

Modern Hebrew literature's engagement with the Bible has always seemed to me to be an engrossing phenomenon, not merely as a literary topos, but as a major influence in the shaping of Israel's modern identity. Linguistically, it is of singular interest, since it is made possible by, and indeed perpetuates, the temporal polyphony that is Hebrew. A new-ancient language, Hebrew is an ongoing palimpsest, both written and spoken, in which subliminal layers show through and are sounded rather than subsumed. This property of the language challenges the modern writer to employ the diachronic dictionary of Hebrew as if it were synchronic, and may therefore be seen as either an empowering property or a handicap. In any case, in this state of affairs, texts are almost doomed to become intertextual. Such condensation may be ascribed, in part, to the natural condensation of tenses that exists in Hebrew and, in part, to the unique history of the language, in which the Bible has played more than a stationary role.

Hebrew's miraculous revival from a language living almost solely in texts to a spoken everyday language took place within a span of no more than a hundred years or so. For immediate resources, the revival had to draw on textual models and storehouses, first and foremost among which was the Bible—a choice governed not least by the Bible's central role in Zionist ideology. For a people returning to its homeland, the Bible served as a title deed, a legal document of ownership. It was to be a historical and political model for the new-revived Jewish kingdom. At the same time it became the focal point for the people's disappointments and frustrations with the promised land. My first chapter, therefore, shows the fascination that the biblical myth holds for the modern Israeli poet and tries to trace the link between the psychological roots of the collective experience and stylistic phenomena—especially those stylistic features natural to the language that allow the special fusion between past and present to take place. It seemed natural, therefore, to focus this study on poetry, a genre whose protagonist, as it were, is language itself.

Continuing these considerations in the second and third chapters, I attempt to draw a stereoscopic map of biblical intertextuality in modern Hebrew poetry from the historical, rhetorical, and feminist points of view. Each of the two chapters introduces one major type of intertextual reading: chapter two takes the story of the Binding of Isaac and its metamorphoses as a test case for studying the history of modern Hebrew poetry and Hebrew literariness and, consequently, also looks at intertextuality as a critical tool for investigating historical change. Chapter three deals with intertextuality in women's poetry as a strategy for constructing a modern feminine identity. Both are eclectic in their methodology, with structuralist and intertextual theoretical premises. All three chapters, though united by the theme of intertextuality, may be read independently as studies in practical interpretation.

The book is based on the Gustave A. and Mamie W. Efroymson Memorial Lectures delivered at Hebrew Union College in March 1995. Of course I have expanded the material presented in the lectures and added bibliographical references. I would like to thank my hosts for all the kindness shown to me during my stay in Cincinnati. Thanks are also due to my attentive and well-informed audiences, from whose questions and comments I derived much benefit. My thanks go to the Hebrew Union College Press, especially to Dr. Michael A. Meyer and the editor Barbara Selya, for the work they invested in the manuscript and their professional manner throughout. My friends and colleagues Dr. Ada Rapapport-Albert of University College, London, and Professor Malachi Beit-Arié of the Hebrew University, Jerusalem, bestowed on the manuscript a blend of generosity and tough-mindedness that greatly improved it. My gratitude also goes to the Master and Fellows of St. John's College, Cambridge, especially to the President, Dr. A. Macintosh, who invited me to spend three months as a visiting scholar to work on the project.

The nucleus of the thesis presented in the chapter on the Binding of Isaac appeared in *Prooftexts* (Johns Hopkins University Press, September 1988). All references to the Bible are to the 1611 Authorized Version, unless otherwise indicated. The translations of the poems are acknowledged in the footnotes.

The Prophet's Tongue in Our Cheek
The Bible as the Intimate Other

Introduction

In a few thoughtful remarks on his magnum opus, *Mr. Mani*, A.B. Yehoshua offers a glimpse of personal history as an interpretive key to the novel. He reveals that from early childhood, when accompanying his father to the synagogue on Rosh Hashanah, he has been troubled by the myth of the Binding of Isaac: "It hovers like a black bird over our lives," he says. "Through this novel I hoped to rid myself, and the collective self, of this highly significant and terrifying myth [i.e. the myth of a father who is prepared to sacrifice his son], which weighs so heavily upon our history."[1]

How should this be done? "What was merely a threat in the biblical story will materialize into a terrible reality in my novel. If I enact the threat I may be able to empty it of its magic and extract the life out of the narrative. I call this eradicating the Aqedah through its realization."[2] In his confession, therefore, A.B. Yehoshua takes issue with the biblical model and brings to it his secular interpretations.

I wonder whether there is any other modern secular culture whose dialogue with its own scriptures is so argumentative, angry, and intense as that in contemporary Hebrew literature. To engage in this dialogue is not an option but a must; the choices are of an existential magnitude. From this point of view, the position of the great intertext in modern Hebrew and Israeli secular culture is unique. Debate and polemic are inherent in the deep psychic structure of Jewish culture. Indeed, in contemporary Hebrew literature, the Scriptures do not function as a unifying myth, but rather as a battleground for contest and argument. The relationship with the Bible is one of conflict.

Yet, however iconoclastic modern Israeli poets are, they do not try to erase the ancient intertext by ignoring it. Their strategy is to distance themselves from it, thereby making its presence more pervasive and intrusive. The more the intertext is wrestled with, the more acutely it is felt. As in every act of rebellion, the opponent becomes the focus, since one places at the center precisely that which one wishes to push aside.

However, it is only when myth is rooted in a domestic language and becomes, so to speak, family property that it can function as a battleground. The closer one lives to the myth, the more likely one is to quarrel with it and consequently to assume responsibility for it. As a family dispute, modern Hebrew's quarrel with the Bible readily lends itself to interpretation in terms of the Bloomian oedipal model of literary history.

Bloom views literary history as a family romance; as an oedipal conflict between strong poets: "Poetic strength," he says in *A Map of Misreading,* "comes only from a triumphant wrestling with the greatest of the dead."[3] In his elaboration of a theory of influence, Bloom focuses on an interpersonal— and imaginary—relationship between strong poets, positing catastrophe as the "central element in poetic imagination."[4]

In Hebrew and Israeli literature we find that generally the strong poet in this conflict is replaced by strong language. The oedipal conflict takes place in the linguistic arena. The agonistic struggle with precursors is replaced by the struggle with the Scriptures. It is a struggle of male and female poets with an authoritative text or with the models derived from it.

Yehuda Amichai speaks openly about the problem of "belatedness." He wonders how, confronted with such a vast and seemingly complete tradition, a poet may use its materials to produce a work that is recognizable as belonging to that tradition as well as being unique in its own right: "The struggle with the heritage of my forefathers begins with waking, / It robs me of all my energy."

The confrontation of modern Hebrew literature with the biblical text is distinct from the traditional Jewish posture towards the Bible. Responding to Harold Bloom's model in *Anxiety of Influence,* David Stern, in his *Midrash and Theory,* observes:

> The response the Rabbis made to these doubts about their election, about the authority of their tradition, was to adopt an interpretive posture that represents the very opposite of Harold Bloom's idea of the anxiety of influence. The Rabbis consciously—happily, we might say—assume the stance of belatedness. Precisely what they seek to prove is that all innovations and intentions of their tradition can already be found in the text of the Bible, that nothing they say is original; hence the essential preoccupation of Midrash is with finding in the biblical text a source for every law and belief in Rabbinic tradition, no matter how contrived the connection may be.[5]

In contrast to the midrashic tradition, modern Israeli poets use biblical quotations, allusions, fragmentary phrases or words for the purpose of expressing not only their spiritual debt to the great intertext but mainly their sense of distance and alienation from it. In many cases, then, a desire for distance from the mode of imitation prompts Israeli poets to exercise literary violence upon the biblical text through misreading and rewriting. This is how Israeli poets convey their particular "anxiety of influence."

After the 1982 Israeli war in Lebanon, in which her son was killed, Ra'aya Harnik, a contemporary Israeli poet, wrote:

אֲנִי לֹא אַקְרִיב
בְּכוֹרִי לְעוֹלָה
לֹא אֲנִי

בַּלֵּילוֹת אֱלֹהִים וַאֲנִי
עוֹרְכִים חֶשְׁבּוֹנוֹת
מַה מַּגִּיעַ לְמִי

אֲנִי יוֹדַעַת וּמַכִּירָה
תּוֹדָה.
אֲבָל לֹא אֶת בְּנִי
וְלֹא
לְעוֹלָה.

I will not offer
My first born for sacrifice
Not I

At night God and I
Make reckonings
Who can claim what

I know and am
Grateful
But not my son
And not
for sacrifice[6]

It is through distancing herself from the family archive, from the model of the Binding of Isaac, that Harnik makes a political statement. The rhetorical strategy is the total negation of the biblical הִנֵּנִי ("Here I am")–the readiness, the absolute obedience of the scriptural Abraham. Indeed, much of the political poetry written in Israel since the 1970s–and especially in the 1980s, after the war in Lebanon–is concerned with stating what it is not; proposing itself as "not x" where x is a biblical intertextual referent.

This rhetorical strategy of much of contemporary Israeli poetry can be defined, in the wake of Johathan Culler, as "negative presupposition," e.g., a poem describes what something is not in order to distance itself from another form of poetic discourse.[7]

In Israeli literature, the use of negative presupposition must be seen not merely as a rhetorical or ornamental device. It differs from the *litotes*, which employs deliberate understatement for purposes of intensification or affirmation by the negativity of the contrary. While the *litotes* designates rhetorical purposes and semantic effects, the negative presupposition is a psychological stance; it is charged with anger and emotion. It is a denial of what one wants to rid oneself of. The poet speaks in the name of motherhood and in the name of all mothers. She places herself above the divine decree, as if saying "I will not give in and you will not force me to submit." Moreover, negative presupposition can be used as a tool for defining cultural space. When the poet says, "I will not offer my first born for sacrifice," she relates not only to the past twenty or thirty years of Israeli Zionist history; what she attempts to deconstruct is an ancient and continuous model. Negative presupposition is therefore a precise marker of cultural memory—a map, a yardstick for defining identity. Collective cultural memory turns into personal memory. The question is always: In relation to what does one define one's own identity? In Israeli culture the Bible becomes the *intimate other*. The desire to step out of history is therefore expressed within the family language.

This negative presupposition is described in the following pages by means of an intertextual methodology. Indeed, the intertextual method is an effective tool by which to explain the synchronic status of the Bible in modern Israeli literature. According to intertextual theories, no text is a closed entity. All discourse occurs in dialogue with some other discourses, which precede it chronologically and/or ontologically. Intertextuality is also a notion of conflict. "In proposing itself as 'not x,' where x is the intertextual reference, a text claims literary status for itself but simultaneously distinguishes itself as a negativity with respect to the canon, and in so doing also distances itself from socially marked discourse that nevertheless necessarily traverses it."[8]

Biblical intertextuality plays a major part in Israeli literature and has a politically subversive nature. The "not I" is often a biblical referent. The resulting paradoxical process is that the dispute revives the negated intertext more effectively than the simple narrative technique of filling in the psychological and narrative gaps in the biblical text. But during this process, the intertext (the text referred to)[9] does not remain untouched. The concept underlying intertextuality is that the intertext may be harmed by the intertextual relationship. The encounter with the modern literary text transforms the understanding of the biblical narrative for the contemporary reader. This rereading of the text is not only an assault on the original biblical text; it is also the triumph of the Bible. The hermeneutic function is reversed and becomes reciprocal: lock turns into key, key into lock.

Nevertheless, the great intertext is not merely a protected library in Borges's sense of the word, but a concrete historical reality (When Pierre Menar plays games, he does it in the convenient and protected reality of the library. His games have no historical projections). Many of the referents in modern Hebrew literature represent what Edward Said has called "the worldly aspects of the text. The human and social conditions which are implied in it."[10] I would argue that the Midrash is more like a library, while for modern Hebrew literature, history and the world are a dominant frame of reference.

How the Diachronic Becomes Synchronic: Mixing Registers

The intimate and quarrelsome dialogue with the Hebrew Bible in modern Israeli literature is possible not only because of the historical parallels between the ancient narrative and contemporary reality that converge in the same geographical space, but also because of the unique position of the Hebrew language–the fact that in Modern Hebrew there is no difference between the synchronic and the diachronic dictionary; that Modern Hebrew words can be used in both the contemporary and the ancient registers and so burden even the so-called colloquial register with various associations and connotations of three thousand years of semantic history. Moreover, since the Bible is a part of the Israeli code, the poet can also rely on the fact that the addressee will be able to recapture the multilayered information. One can say, therefore, that there are many competent readers within the Israeli reading public.

Each transition from literary Hebrew to the spoken language sheds new light on the great intertext. The poem 'רֶגַע אֶחָד' ("One Moment") by Natan Zach, the precursor of the vernacular in Israeli poetry, which opens his revolutionary volume, שירים שונים ("Various Poems," 1960) is a great example of modern eulogy and exemplifies this process. In it Zach uses historical lapses as a time tunnel. The imaginary dialogue between the living and the dead is represented through the surrealist proximity of past and present, thus transforming the traditional genre of eulogy into a modernistic idiom that is psychoanalytically informed.

לאסיה

רֶגַע אֶחָד שֶׁקֶט בְּבַקָּשָׁה. אָנָּא. אֲנִי
רוֹצֶה לוֹמַר דְּבַר מָה. הוּא הָלַךְ
וְעָבַר עַל פָּנַי. יָכֹלְתִּי לָגַעַת בְּשׁוּלֵי
אַדַּרְתּוֹ. לֹא נָגַעְתִּי. מִי יָכוֹל הָיָה
לָדַעַת מַה שֶׁלֹּא יָדָעְתִּי.

הֶחָול דָּבַק בִּבְגָדָיו. בִּזְקָנו
הִסְתַּבְּכוּ זְרָדִים. כַּנִּרְאֶה לָן
לַיְלָה קֹדֶם בַּתֶּבֶן. מִי יָכוֹל הָיָה
לָדַעַת שֶׁבְּעוֹד לַיְלָה יִהְיֶה
רֵיק כְּמוֹ צִפּוֹר, קָשֶׁה כְּמוֹ אֶבֶן.

לֹא יָכֹלְתִּי לָדַעַת. אֵינֶנִּי מַאֲשִׁים
אוֹתוֹ. לִפְעָמִים אֲנִי מַרְגִּישׁ אוֹתוֹ קָם
בִּשְׁנָתוֹ, סַהֲרוּרִי כְּמוֹ יָם, חוֹלֵף לְיָדִי, אוֹמֵר
לִי בְּנִי.
בְּנִי. לֹא יָדַעְתִּי שֶׁאַתָּה, בְּמִדָּה כָּזֹאת, אִתִּי.

For Assia

Quiet for a moment. Please. I'd like to
say something. He went away and
passed in front of me. I could have
touched the hem of his cloak. I didn't.
Who could have known what I didn't
know.

There was sand stuck to his clothes.
Sprigs were tangled in his beard. He
must have slept on straw the night
before. Who could have known that in
Another night he would be hollow as a
bird, hard as a stone.

I could not have known. I don't blame
him. Sometimes I feel him getting up
in his sleep, moonstruck like the sea,
flitting by me, saying to me my son.
My son. I didn't know that you are, to
such an extent, with me.[11]

Any English translation, however accurate, is bound to disappoint, simply
because the English colloquial is free from the enormous bulk weighing
down every tendon of spoken Hebrew. No foreign tongue can accurately
transmit Zach's almost neurotic consciousness of the Hebrew language as a
palimpsest.

Nothing in English discloses that the innocent sounding comment הוּא הָלַךְ
וַעֲבַר עַל פָּנַי ("he went away and passed in front of me") is in fact secreting a
moment of epiphany in Jewish history, a moment that dramatizes the eter-

nal war between the abstract and the concrete in monotheism. It is an allusion to Exodus 34:6, where God, descending in the cloud on Mount Sinai, "passes in front of Moses" (וַיַּעֲבֹר ... עַל־פָּנָיו). None of my students has ever raised an eyebrow on hearing this line. It seems to them an integral part of everyday Israeli speech. The allusion is so hushed, so barefacedly guileless, precisely because it is an expression used every day: "He passed by."

But Zach, ever a guileful poet, camouflages the allusion by a subtle alteration: he changes the biblical tense of וַיַּעֲבֹר (future inverted into past of the root עב"ר: "pass") by means of the characteristic slight of hand of the *vav conversive* (ו"ו ההיפוך). (The biblical conversive *vav* reverses a structure in the future tense into the past tense). In Zach's poem the past is definitely past, serving to mark the chasm between the dead father and the living son. No longer can the past dwell in tense unison with the future as in the biblical tense. Thus Hebrew allows the revisionist writing to occur not only through structural changes of quotations and references but within the words and tenses themselves.

The further insertion of הוּא הָלַךְ (translated here "he went away") is also colloquial Hebrew for "passed away, gone." The use of enjambment in הָלַךְ/ וְעָבַר emphasizes the use of הָלַךְ, which is now separated from its natural partner עָבַר, to signify something different, namely the colloquial meaning of הָלַךְ ("died"), without losing the sense of הָלַךְ וְעָבַר as an acceptable collocation for the verb "to pass by." The phrase הוּא הָלַךְ וְעָבַר עַל פָּנַי has survived not as a quotation but as a speech form. The past exists in the very matrix of the language.

The next step is the mention of the ancient term אַדֶּרֶת ("cloak" or "mantle"), not regularly used in modern Hebrew. It carries the reader abruptly from the everyday, mundane setting of informal speech or lecture that usually commences with the words רֶגַע אֶחָד, שֶׁקֶט בְּבַקָּשָׁה. The tantalizing image automatically evoked by the אַדֶּרֶת is that of the heartrending scene before the prophet Elijah departs from his disciple Elisha (II Kings 2:11-14). It hovers above the whole poem from now on. Moreover, the "cloak," which is a transparent allusion, functions as a suspect detail; its presence strongly alerts the reader to the previous somewhat subtle intertextual reference of רָאָה and וְעָבַר. One might argue that the subtlety of Zach's poem emerges from the usually nontransparent, nonquotational reference to the biblical text.

The אַדֶּרֶת is also implied at the end. The poem eulogizes the disappearance of the father—biological or spiritual—and is marked by feelings of guilt, loss, and missed opportunities:

לִפְעָמִים אֲנִי מַרְגִּישׁ אוֹתוֹ קָם

בִּשְׁנָתוֹ, סַהֲרוּרִי כְּמוֹ יָם, חוֹלֵף לְיָדִי, אוֹמֵר

לִי בְּנִי.

בְּנִי. לֹא יָדַעְתִּי שֶׁאַתָּה, בְּמִדָּה כָּזֹאת, אִתִּי.

Sometimes I feel him getting up
in his sleep, moonstruck like the sea,
flitting by me, saying to me my son.
My son. I didn't know that you are, to
such an extent, with me.[12]

Yet the reader, familiar with the canon, cannot help but hear two biblical
cries of mourning: Elisha crying with agony over the departure of his
spiritual father Elijah as he watches him ascending in a whirlwind into
heaven: וְהוּא מְצַעֵק אָבִי אָבִי רֶכֶב יִשְׂרָאֵל וּפָרָשָׁיו "My father, my father, the
chariot of Israel and its horses" (II Kings, 2:12). The other cry of mourning
that resonates here is: "O my son Absalom, O Absalom my son, my son"
(II Samuel 19:1). The juxtaposition of the two cries lends a double identity
to the father—biological and spiritual.

The hidden and intricate dialogue with the biblical text continues. In the
English Bible, when the sons of the prophets ask Elisha: "Knowest thou that
the Lord will take away thy master from thy head today?" Elisha answers:
גַּם־אֲנִי יָדַעְתִּי ("Yea, I know it") The modern poet complains: מי יכול היה לדעת
מה שלא ידעתי "Who could have known / what I did not / know." A human
being cannot predict the actual moment of death. The use of the biblical
crochet "knowest" highlights the glaring difference between modern-day
English and the ancient language. In English it serves as a tag, saying "Here
is ancient stuff." In Hebrew the word remains unaltered.

The use of the ancient canon, its continuity in our consciousness, makes
us partners in mourning. The vehicle for mourning is what used to be a dead
language, sprinkled with the living elements of the vernacular. The dead
language is being revived in much the same way that mourning is a process
of revival. The poem "A Moment" is mourning in its own mirror: the language is the mirror.

Even the very translation of the title 'רֶגַע אֶחָד' presents the issue: "A
moment," as the poet T. Carmi translates, or "one moment," which I would
prefer. "A moment" is more formal, while "one moment," or even its colloquial Hebrew meaning "wait a minute," corresponds to daily speech. Thus
the title, or the opening, places it right away for the Hebrew speaker in an
argumentative register (when you have an argument or dispute you say רֶגַע
אֶחָד); it is also a plea, "wait a minute." It also conjures up the addressee.

The first line therefore sets the poem in the authentic intimate key of quarrel, dispute, laden with guilt feelings, accusation and plea with the dead father ("I don't blame him"), as if between two living people. But simultaneously the archaic language uplifts the father to a monumental stance, like a deity. The phrase רֶגַע אֶחָד, שֶׁקֶט בְּבַקָשָׁה succeeds in conveying an intonation that usually stands outside the framework of the written text. The colloquial expression introduces a single possible choice of intonation, thus investing the text with an "absent quality." While a literary phrase presents its reader with various possible intonations, this colloquial phrase is a sort of "printed voice."

Zach's poem exemplifies the interplay of registers in Hebrew. Unlike English, Hebrew does not expose the grammatical elements of the registers to the reader. In the case of English one has to decide, for example, between "knowest" and "know," thus defining a priori the linguistic register to be employed. In Hebrew the same word can be used in both the ancient and the modern registers simultaneously, burdening even the so-called colloquial register with various associations and connotations of three thousand years of semantic history.

The poet can rely on the fact that his or her addressee will be able to recapture the multilevel information conveyed in the poem, since the Bible is a part of the Israeli code and its readers are well acquainted with a great number of collocations and words such as אַדֶּרֶת. The fact that Hebrew orthography has not changed in two thousand years also enables the writer to use more complex and mixed registers.

The system creates an intricate interlacing relation among registers. Literary modern Hebrew is an aggregate of registers providing the writer with a complex system of associations and connotations. In Hebrew one touches upon latent archetypes and codes through the spoken language itself even where the intertext is not immediately identifiable.

Every poetic moment is, therefore, a balancing act between a stone and a feather. Every transient utterance, the casual, the flat, the superficial, seems to be outweighed by the ancient, while at the same time a miraculous property invested in the feather outweighs the stone.

The Power of Punning/Paronomasia

The intricate interlacing of registers in Hebrew poetry is enhanced by the abundant and creative use of paronomasia as an intertextual strategy.[12] Paronomasia is defined as "A figure in which by means of a modification of sound, or change of letters, a close resemblance to a given verb or noun is produced, so that similar words express dissimilar things."[13]

The root is the most important factor in Hebrew. Each root may generate a large number of verbs and nouns that vary in meaning. Yet the reader is always able to identify the underlying abstract morpheme. The Hebrew reader is normally exposed to phonological as well as semantic ambiguity. The unpointed letters לקח ("take") and לֶקַח ("a moral lesson") seem the same but are semantically distinct, yet the Hebrew reader will be able to identify the common root while processing the printed word. Consequently paronomasia is especially active in a root language.

The issues of register and paronomasia are intertwined. The tension between registers is reflected in the different types of paronomasia inherent in modern Hebrew poetry. Let me take for example the paronomasia מַאֲכֶלֶת ("a knife"), which will be used by Amir Gilboa in his poem "Isaac" (see below p. 51) and אכל ("food, eating"). Hebrew readers will immediately identify the מַאֲכֶלֶת as a murderous tool used in the biblical narrative of the Binding of Isaac. If this word, which so transparently belongs to the biblical register, is introduced by the poet into a modern register, it is likely to foreground the biblical text. The change of context immediately alerts the reader to the root common to both registers—and so brings the root to life.

The context—the convention of poetical reading—calls and invites the reader to identify the common root. After all, the conventions of poetry call the reader to activate a strong yet subtle linguistic awareness. Since modern and ancient Hebrew use the same building blocks—the same roots—the reader can easily transcend time and place and walk freely on the path that lies between old and new. The modern reader is likely to identify older strata of the language through the common root.

Modern Hebrew recognizes two alternative vowel systems: one is the Masoretic system (essentially defective spelling) with some *matres lectionis* that consists of a range of signs (dots) inserted within, above, or below the predominantly consonantal script in which classical Hebrew has been preserved. This system is usually used in poetry. The other is closer to the Greek-Latin tradition of treating a certain number of alphabetical signs as vowels (plene or full spelling), which guide the reader on the pronunciation of each syllable. Modern Hebrew prose writing employs the latter; it integrates some of the vowels in the consonantal units that make up the text. In so doing it aims to ensure that each word is recognized, thus lessening ambiguities. Poetry using the old system leaves the kernel—the root—untouched. No vowel signs are inserted. Only a system of dots and bars surrounds the words. However, they remain very much outsiders. Separating the consonant letters from the vowel points that surround them without being integrated into their flow opens up a new spectrum of meanings and ambiguities.

The vowels added to editions of modern Hebrew poetry are unobtrusive. Since they are secondary, they are not necessarily noticed immediately. The consonants stand out and are perceived first, and so the reader is free to explore the ambiguities in the consonantal skeleton. The defective spelling (חָסֵר) in modern Hebrew poetry exposes the root to the eye. This is not so in prose, where the vowel letters in the full spelling (מָלֵא) make the root a little less obvious.[14]

The significance of this factor cannot be overestimated. As a root language, Hebrew facilitates both explicit and implicit intertextuality of a special kind—one that stems from the productive morphology of the root. Indeed, it is surprising to see how creative the use of different types of paronomasia can be and how, through it, different kinds of narratives can be generated in the poems. Since I would argue together with Kristeva that reading is "aggressive participation,"[15] it seems that these tropes engage the reader in speculative activity—a speculation that centers not around the historical source, but on the signifying force of the paronomasia that has its genesis in the reading process itself.

Through the use of such rhetorical devices, poets are able to free themselves from the arbitrariness and banality of language and to reveal its depth and magic. The following chapters argue that paronomasia and pun serve modern Hebrew poetry not only to bridge registers but to awaken the argumentative facet in the poem. Debate and polemics are thus conducted not only through the confrontation between ideological models but also through the tension between the conscious and the subconscious life of the language itself.

A Double Bind

*The Sacrifice of Isaac as a Paradigm
in Modern Hebrew Poetry*

m. Kadishman.

אותה ונלוה אותו אהב לעקסא.

Introduction

Twentieth-century Jewish history confronts the Hebrew literary imagination with what seems like an astonishing repetition of the biblical drama. The ingathering of the Jews in the modern state of Israel recalls the biblical exodus from Egypt and, later, the return to Zion of the Babylonian exiles. Israel's War of Independence echoes the conquest of the land by Joshua and the judges. The present-day consolidation of the Jewish State has obvious analogies with the Solomonic Kingdom of Israel. The story of Hagar and Ishmael seems to anticipate the present-day conflict with the Arabs. The revolt of Absalom against David might prefigure the tensions between the founding fathers of Israel and their sons. Moreover, the narrative of the Binding of Isaac has become the metaphor for the most cataclysmic event of the twentieth century, the Holocaust.

Clearly, the dialogue with the Bible is not the sole preserve of modern Hebrew literature. Every Hebrew text is necessarily polyphonic. But what is distinctive about this modern dialogue is the inexorable feeling that history seems to be repeating itself, albeit in a new guise, like a film being rerun. Zionism has once more brought the Hebrew poet to the foot of Mount Moriah, and that in itself compels him to view the Binding of Isaac in a light quite different to that of the medieval poet who composed his verse in the Rhine valley. How can Mount Moriah be a stable frame of reference when it still bears witness to so many other trials? The modern Jew is daily reviving the ancient text.[1]

The relationship of the modern secular writer to the biblical text, which history replays, is extremely complex. It involves the simultaneous elaboration of similarities and oppositions through a plethora of devices: quotation and distorted quotation, an aspiration to the sublime and a descent to the ironic, and the mocking sanctification of the profane, which merges with the profanation of the holy. The biblical echoes are used and abused; their powerful allusions are recorded and then subverted through irony. Above all, one always feels the unqualified admiration of the modern artist for the biblical text as a literary creation. From this point of view postmodernism was introduced early into Israeli literature, through the questioning of the great narratives and the ironization of the sublime through intertextuality.

It is possible, then, to study modern Hebrew and Israeli literature in the light of what I have called elsewhere the *re-dramatization* of biblical models.[2] Yet the Binding of Isaac, known in the Hebrew tradition by the term *Aqedah*, derived from the root עק״ד meaning to bind to an altar—and we will keep

17

this term throughout the book—remains indisputably the most prominent and most powerful of all these biblical topoi.

In his classic essay *The Last Trial,* Shalom Spiegel shows the *Aqedah* to be a central text in the Jewish hermeneutic tradition.[3] The personal choices of Abraham, the first of the patriarchs and founder of monotheism, were decisive in shaping the destiny of his descendants. Indeed, the fate of the Jewish people was bound up with Isaac's fate. In the Binding of Isaac, the future hope of Israel—even the stars—were bound in jeopardy. Moreover, the challenge that the biblical tale presents to the literary imagination goes far beyond its historical and religious meanings. Erich Auerbach, in his classic *Mimesis,* speaks of the Hebrew narrative as a text "fraught with background."[4] Its ambiguities and paradoxes, its linguistic duplications and displacements, its unsaid words and unsettling terror cast a spell on the modern poet and invite him to wrestle with them. As a result, the story has become the progenitor of an entire tradition of Western narrative technique.

The prominence of the story in religious tradition is understandable. What is surprising is its persistence, bordering on obsession, in secular modern Hebrew and Israeli literature. Secularization has deprived modern Hebrew literature of two of the main traditional, theological motifs of the *Aqedah*: love for God, and the covenant with Him. This has had two principal ramifications: first, in the modern adaptations of the *Aqedah,* the relationship between man and God is gradually replaced, first by the relationship between man (either as an individual or nation) and his socio-historical circumstances, and then by the relationship between man and his self, his own existence, his fate. Secondly, by turning the *Aqedah* into a secular story, the modern poet liberates himself from the constraints of the biblical text. He is thus able to amplify the semantic range of the original words and concepts, sometimes reaching the point at which this playful engagement with familiar biblical phrases becomes macabre. One of the principles of this technique is the juxtaposition of ancient biblical episodes with the here and now, so that both are viewed from a level perspective, as if taking place simultaneously. In this way the story of the *Aqedah* becomes the means by which the sublime may be deflated by irony, and its deflation comes to define the here and now.

Admittedly, the response to contemporary events through the biblical narrative of the *Aqedah* is characteristic of earlier works in the religious tradition. This is a feature, for example, of liturgical poems that were written in reaction to the pogroms at the time of the Crusades. Yet the response at the time was still wholly subordinate to the theme of the relationship between God and man, the relationship of covenant and martyrdom.

As mentioned before, the narrative of the *Aqedah* is no less central in modern Hebrew literature than it was in the Hebrew culture of the past. There is scarcely a poet who does not use or abuse this narrative in his work. Indeed, a vast anthology of such poems could be compiled. The biblical archetype provides the modern secular poet with relevant models for the interpretation of historical reality and the self.

Writers of modern Hebrew literature have recreated for their readers this myth, which acts as a sort of critique for all political and social changes and developments. It has become a reservoir of metaphors of contemporary reality. The *Aqedah* is one of the paradigms, possibly the central one, that governs our lives and invests them with meaning—a kind of basic model by which we act. Understanding the dynamics of the *Aqedah* is therefore important not only for a historical understanding of our culture, but also for the identification of the deep structures that have shaped Israeli society and exposed its national trauma. It lays bare the secrets of the collective Israeli psyche.

I have therefore chosen to use the *Aqedah* as a test case for tracing the evolution of the literary and moral discourse of twentieth-century Hebrew poetry. My intention is not to be all-inclusive or to provide a panoramic map, but to focus on major trends in the development of modern Hebrew poetry.[5]

The paradigm of the biblical tale focuses on the encounter between a God who wants proof of his devotee Abraham's faith, and an Abraham who is prepared to suspend both parental love and ethical impulses in order to sacrifice his son to prove his loyalty and religious faith. Isaac, the passive victim, is saved, and a ram is sacrificed in his place. There are four roles or functions (*actants* in Greimas' terminology)[6] in the biblical narrative: 1. the author of the command to sacrifice Isaac; 2. the one who binds; 3. the one who is bound; 4. the ultimate victim. Every generation produces the drama afresh: the roles remain the same, but the characters change. In order to use intertextuality as a tool for detecting the dynamism of historical change and to trace both the history of twentieth-century Hebrew poetry and the development of Hebrew literariness, I shall examine who occupies the different roles at different stages of history and the transformation of roles wrought upon the biblical narrative. As in any structuralist model, the same function (actant) can be manifested by more than one character, and the same character can be assigned more than one function. Moreover, it should be em-

m. Kadishman.

phasized that not all the four participants are simultaneously present in any one poem. In some cases, only a few elements recreate the atmosphere of the *Aqedah.*

Needless to say, an entire midrashic and exegetical literature stretches across the expanse that lies between the Bible and modern Hebrew literature. I have chosen a primarily structural methodology based upon the principle of *transformation* (in Hebrew הַמְרָה) because it also echoes the canonical exegetical tradition of the *Aqedah,* which emphasizes the substitution of the ram for Isaac. Spiegel emphasizes that the idea of transformation is central to midrashic interpretation. Indeed, the talmudic sages (Pesikta R 40) suggest this as an etymological explanation for the name of the mountain: "What is the meaning of Moriah? *Temurah,* a substitute offering, an exchange."[7] The moral dimension of the *Aqedah,* for example, stems from the idea of exchanging animal for man. The intertextual structural methods I use here are similarly based on the concept of exchange and transformation.

The Author of the Command

In the poetry of the beginning of the twentieth century, secularization transforms the originator of the command, and God is replaced by an entity less well-defined—by something akin to Jewish history. In the first stage, history replaces theology. As the author of the command, this entity has two dimensions: a past that epitomizes the national experience of unending suffering and destruction, and a future that suggests that the Jewish people are fated to be sacrificed again and again. In this context two additional subtexts may be discerned: the futility of denying the Jewish past, and the yearning for Jewish redemption—the latter primarily expressed in a Zionism that, as a result of the Jewish return to their land, renews the encounter with sacrifice through a constant struggle for survival in a hostile geopolitical environment. The God who gives the command is thus replaced by two substitutes: national destiny and the idea of rebirth. The transformation did not take place overnight, and in the intermediate stage there was still a dialogue with God, the original author of the command. But the religious motif of God's testing of Abraham, the very foundation of the earlier literature of the *Aqedah,* gradually began to disappear.

The 1920s marked a turning point when the center of Hebrew literature shifted from Europe to Jewish Palestine. The God who tests now plays a lesser role, and His position is increasingly replaced by a prevailing sense of historical destiny and Zionist commitment. By some fateful historical inertia, even the names of the poets begin to play tricks of identity: Abraham

Shlonsky identifies with his patriarchal namesake as does the poet Rachel with her matriarchal namesake. An especially interesting case is that of the poet Yocheved Shlezniak who, at the age of seventeen names herself בַּת־מִרְיָם, by which she designates herself a poet. Once, she explained, Bialik called all Hebrew women poets בְּנוֹת מִרְיָם (daughters of Miriam). The new name is an inversion of the biblical order—Miriam, the biblical poet, was daughter to Yocheved, the mother of Moses. For the new Hebrew poet, poetry takes the parental place. In a sense, it becomes the parent of parenthood.

We look first at the poet Yitzhak Lamdan (1899-1954), a central figure in the poetry of the third *Aliyah* (wave of immigration). When Yitzhak Lamdan identifies himself with his biblical namesake, he does not have in mind the individual Isaac, in accordance with the ideological code of his generation, but rather with a representative and collective Isaac, a sort of יִצְחָקִיּוּת, if you like. In a poem entitled 'עַל הַמִּזְבֵּחַ' ("On the Altar"), he writes:

פֹּה כֻּלָּנוּ עֲקֻדְנוּ וּבְמוֹ יָדֵינוּ הֵבֵאנוּ הֲלוֹם הָעֵצִים,
וְאַל שְׁאוֹל וְחָקֹר אִם תֵּרָצֶה הָעוֹלָה!
נַפְשִׁיל, אֵפוֹא, דּוּמָם צַוָּאר עַל הַמִּזְבֵּחַ:

We are all bound here, and with our own hands we brought the wood here.
And don't ask if the sacrifice will be accepted!...
Just let us stretch our neck silently at the altar.[8]

The passive word "accepted" registers the poet's uncertainty as to who is to do the accepting and whom to address. However, all of Lamdan's essentially pessimistic poetry is replete with images of patriotic self-sacrifice and the archetype of collective suicide on Massada (he is the author of 'מַסָּדָה', one of the epic poems that shaped the master narrative of Zionism). The line "with our own hands we brought the wood" should be taken literally. The reclaiming of the land and the planting of trees are now the referent of command. In the modern *Aqedah* the wood is no longer just fuel. It becomes an important part of the claiming of the land. Though its carrier may still be crushed by his load, the load itself becomes a symbol of, indeed a means to, the establishment of collective norms. Here the narrative of the *Aqedah* helps create the persona of the victim-martyr in the consciousness of the yishuv, portrayed as a hero of settlement and struggle who falls in battle and unites with the soil of his country.

In contrast to the biblical archetype, he who is bound now chooses his own fate and is wholly conscious of it. Thus, until the 1950s and 1960s, poems employing the *Aqedah* myth expressed a sense of a shared fate, a collective, even mystical concept of Jewish destiny, the roots of which lay in the literature at the beginning of the century in the works of such writers as Berdyczewski, Yaacov Cohen, and others.

The same collective experience is also dominant in the poetry of the generation of the War of Independence, also known as the Palmach generation, the first native-born Israelis. Here again, the collective nature of the act of sacrifice was never more important. The reader in the pre-state yishuv, preparing for the War of Independence, anticipated the plot based on the heroic ritual of sacrifice. Literature and theater alike played a cathartic role in facilitating the ritual of the actual sacrifice. During the War of Independence a large number of plots in Israeli drama ended with the death of the hero, whose sacrificial action enabled society to go on living. Such rituals were to accompany Hebrew literature for a long while, and the evolution of Hebrew writing is reflected in the changing attitudes to this ritual of sacrifice.[9]

There is no individual martyr in ʼיְרֻשָּׁה ("Heritage") by Haim Gouri, the most renowned representative of the Palmach generation. Instead, the Jewish future is bound.

הָאַיִל בָּא אַחֲרוֹן.
וְלֹא יָדַע אַבְרָהָם כִּי הוּא
מֵשִׁיב לִשְׁאֵלַת הַיֶּלֶד,
רֵאשִׁית־אוֹנוֹ בְּעֵת יוֹמוֹ עָרָב.

נָשָׂא רֹאשׁוֹ הַשָּׂב.
בִּרְאוֹתוֹ כִּי לֹא חָלַם חֲלוֹם
וְהַמַּלְאָךְ נִצָּב-
נָשְׁרָה הַמַּאֲכֶלֶת מִיָּדוֹ.

הַיֶּלֶד שֶׁהֻתַּר מֵאֲסוּרָיו
רָאָה אֶת גַּב אָבִיו.

יִצְחָק, כַּמְסֻפָּר, לֹא הֹעֲלָה קָרְבָּן.
הוּא חַי יָמִים רַבִּים,
רָאָה בַּטּוֹב, עַד אוֹר עֵינָיו כָּהָה.

אֲבָל אֶת הַשָּׁעָה הַהִיא הוֹרִישׁ לְצֶאֱצָאָיו.
הֵם נוֹלָדִים
וּמַאֲכֶלֶת בְּלִבָּם.

The ram came last of all.
And Abraham did not know that it came
To answer the boy's question —
First of his strength when his day was on the wane.

The old man raised his head.
Seeing that it was no dream
And that the angel stood there—
The knife slipped from his hand

The boy, released from his bonds,
Saw his father's back.

Isaac, as the story goes, was not sacrificed.
He lived for many years,
Saw what pleasure had to offer, until his eyesight dimmed.

But he bequeathed that hour to his offspring.
They are born
With a knife in their hearts.[10]

At this stage, history issues the command. Nothing happens to Isaac, but his trauma becomes his heritage—his children inherit its memory as a kind of genetic code. Gouri visualizes Jewish history as a sort of relay race in which the knife in the heart is a kind of eternal baton. The continuity of a traumatic existence is the destiny of the Jews. The ideal of historical continuity replaces traditional faith. Wars are viewed on the continuum of Jewish history. In that unbroken line of bindings there are gaps and there are those who escape their fate, as did Isaac himself. Every runner in the race is therefore both a son and a father. Here we encounter the typical modern reversal of the conclusive character of the *Aqedah* as found in traditional religious interpretations.[11] The test is now a perpetual recurrence, both of national and of personal history.

Meaning is created here through linguistic intertextuality. A subversive voice of protest is heard through the coupling in Hebrew of the words יְרוּשָׁה ("an inheritance") and לָרֶשֶׁת ("to inherit"), a standard biblical term signifying the national possession of the land, with לְהוֹרִישׁ, which may mean in biblical etymology "to expel or destroy." Through paronomasia the poem associates the command to inherit the land with the Binding of Isaac. The historical right to the land is purchased with pain. Gouri creates an inversion in the function of the poem's title: the concept of inheritance undergoes a symbolic transformation from a positive value to the curse of blood, which hangs like a shadow over the descendants of Isaac. Zionism is a perpetual *Aqedah*.

Different intertextual strategies are activated here. The visual signifier of the biblical text functions as a "siren signifier," to borrow Roland Barthes' terminology: "The intertext is not necessarily a field of influences; rather it is a music of figures, metaphors, thought and words; it is the signifier as siren."[12] The words take on a new life in new contexts but retain the character of loans. The root רא״ה ("to see") appears several times in the biblical narrative. Gouri develops the semantic potentials of this root: "seeing that it was no dream"; "saw his father's back"; "saw what pleasure had to offer, until his eyesight dimmed." He also develops the linguistic doubling in the biblical text–which links רָאָה ("see") and יִרְאָה ("fear"). This latent paronomasia creates an atmosphere of anxiety throughout the poem. Isaac can see only his father's back, and not his face or eyes. The result is a final, irreconcilable break between father and son, brought on by guilt (further increased by the gentler use of the term "boy" rather than "lad"). Two overlapping layers of guilt feelings are present, that of Abraham and that of Isaac. The fiercest guilt appertains to Isaac, who "saw what pleasure had to offer, until his eyesight dimmed."

Read within the context of the Holocaust, the guilt in the poem 'יְרוּשָׁה' can be interpreted as that experienced most acutely by those who were there but survived, and also by those who, placed elsewhere by fate, escaped the catastrophe (Haim Gouri was himself involved in bringing survivors to Israel). What is implicit is the loss of (in)sight–the impossibility of ever comprehending the horror.

No less important than this dialogue with the biblical text is the dialogue between literary generations of "strong poets" contending against one another, and thus affecting the literary evolution of twentieth-century Hebrew poetry. Gouri's מַאֲכֶלֶת בַּלֵּב ("knife in the heart") speaks directly to 'עַל הַיֶּלֶד אַבְרָם' from 'הַטּוּר הַשְּׁבִיעִי' ("The Seventh Column") by Nathan Alterman, whose ethos profoundly influenced the Palmach Generation. This ballad, written in 1943, was inspired by a newspaper article about a child named Avram who slept on the staircase because he was afraid to return to his own bed, despite the pleadings of the shadows of his murdered parents. For Gouri, destiny dictates the fate of the victims, but Alterman elevates the status of the sacrifice, investing it with heroic significance. The dead, from their transcendental sphere, motivate the national resurrection:

בהיותו ישן על מדרגות ביתו בפולין, כתם המלחמה, מפחד לשכב במטתו

עִיר פּוֹלָנִית.
יָרֵחַ רָם.
וּכְתָמִיד - עֲנָנִים בְּשַׁיִט
בְּבוֹא-לַיְלָה שׁוֹכֵב זֶה הַיֶּלֶד אַבְרָם

עַל אַבְנֵי מַדְרֵגוֹת הַבַּיִת.

מִתְיַצֶּבֶת אִמּוֹ לְפָנָיו מִקָּרוֹב
וּבְרַגְלֶיהָ בָּאָרֶץ אֵינֶנָּה נוֹגַעַת.
וְאוֹמֶרֶת: אַבְרָם, קַר הַלַּיִל וְרָטֹב.
בֵּיתָה בּוֹא, לַמִּטָּה הַמְצַעַת.

וְעוֹנֶה לָהּ אַבְרָם:
אִמִּי, אִמִּי,
לֹא אִישַׁן בַּמִּטָּה כְּכָל יֶלֶד.
כִּי אוֹתָךְ בָּהּ רָאִיתִי,
אִמִּי, אִמִּי,
יְשֵׁנָה וּבִלְבֵּךְ מַאֲכֶלֶת.

מִתְיַצֵּב אָז אָבִיו וּמוֹשִׁיט אֵלָיו יָד
וְגוֹעֵר בּוֹ, שָׁקוּף וְגָבוֹהַּ.
וְאוֹמֵר לוֹ: אַבְרָם, בּוֹא הַבַּיְתָה מִיָּד
בְּנִי אַבְרָם, חִישׁ הַבַּיְתָה בּוֹאָה.

וְעוֹנֶה לוֹ אַבְרָם:
אָבִי, אָבִי,
שָׁם אֵפָחֵד לַעֲצֹם הָעֵינַיִם.
כִּי אוֹתְךָ שָׁם רָאִיתִי,
אָבִי, אָבִי,
דָּם יָשֵׁן, בְּלִי רֹאשְׁךָ עַל כְּתֵפַיִם.

אָז נִצֶּבֶת מוּלוֹ אֲחוֹתוֹ הַקְּטַנָּה
וְקוֹרֵאת לוֹ הַבַּיְתָה בְּבֶכִי.
אַךְ עוֹנֶה לָהּ אַבְרָם: שָׁמָּה אַתְּ יְשֵׁנָה
עִם דִּמְעַת הַמֵּתִים עַל לֶחִי.

לְפָנָיו מִתְיַצְּבוֹת אָז שִׁבְעִים הָאֻמּוֹת
וְאוֹמְרוֹת:
הִנְנוּ עָלֶיךָ!
בְּשִׁבְעִים פְּקֻדּוֹת־חֹק וְשִׁבְעִים קַרְדֻּמּוֹת
אֶל הַבַּיִת הַזֶּה נְשִׁיבְךָ!

וְאוֹתְךָ בַּמִּטָּה הַמְצַעַת נַנִּיחָה
וְיָשַׁנְתָּ בָּהּ דֹּם דָּם כְּאָבִיךָ!

וְאַבְרָם בַּחֲלוֹם
צוֹעֵק "אָבִי!"
וְקוֹרֵא שֵׁם אִמּוֹ וְעוֹנָה הִיא:
בְּנִי, אַשְׁרַי... כִּי לוּלֵא הַשַּׁכִּין בְּלִבְּבִי,

לְבָבִי בִּי נִשְׁבַּר לִשְׁנָיִם.

אָז בַּלֵּיל הָשְׁלַךְ הָס
וְיָרֵחַ הוּעַם,
וּמוּל בְּרַק פְּגִיוֹנוֹת שׁוֹחֲרִים לַצַּיִד,
הָיָה דְּבַר אֲדֹנָי אֶל אַבְרָם. אֶל אַבְרָם
הַיָּשֵׁן בִּפְרוֹזְדּוֹר הַבַּיִת.

לֵאמֹר: אַל תִּירָא,
אַל תִּירָא, אַבְרָם,
כִּי גָדוֹל וְעָצוּם אֲשִׂימֶךָ.
לֶךְ לְךָ, דֶּרֶךְ לֵיל מַאֲכֶלֶת דָּם,
אֶל הָאָרֶץ אֲשֶׁר אַרְאֶךָּ.

לֶךְ לְךָ, דֶּרֶךְ לֵיל מַאֲכֶלֶת דָּם.
כַּחַיָּה, כַּתוֹלָע, כַּצִּפּוֹר
מְבָרְכֶיךָ אֲנִי אֲבָרֵךְ, אַבְרָהָם,
וּמְקַלְלֶיךָ אָאֹר.

****

— כָּךְ. לַפֶּרֶק הַזֶּה בְּקוֹרוֹת־הָעִתִּים
שֵׁם קָרָא בָּעוֹלָם: בְּעָיַת הַפְּלִיטִים!
אַךְ לֹא זוֹ הַבְּעָיָה,
לַבְלָרִים בְּנֵי חַיִל...
וְלֹא הִיא הַקּוֹרַעַת תִּיקִים וָתֵיל!

וְלֹא הִיא מוֹלִיכָה הַסְּפִינוֹת אֱלֵי יָם!
כִּי מוֹלִיךְ אוֹתָן רַעַם עַתִּיק וְגָבֹהַּ,
כִּי מוֹלִיךְ אוֹתָן צַו לְדוֹרָיו שֶׁל הָעָם
כִּי מוֹלִיךְ אוֹתָן דְּבַר אֲדֹנָי אֶל אַבְרָם.

**

— וַיֶּחֱרַד אַבְרָהָם וַיִּפֹּל עַל פָּנָיו
וַיֵּצֵא מִנִּי בֵּית וָשַׁעַר.
כִּי הַצַּו שֶׁרָעַם עַל אַבְרָם הָאָב
רוֹעֵם עַל אַבְרָם הַנַּעַר.

(Sleeping on the front steps of his house in Poland at the end of the war, for fear of lying in his bed).

A Polish town,
A risen moon,
As ever the clouds are sweeping.

The boy Avram at nightfall
On the stone front steps sits sleeping.

His mother appears before him
Her feet not touching the earth
And says: Avram, the night is cold and damp.
Come home to your warm clean bed.

And Avram replies:
Oh, Mother, Mother,
In my bed I will not sleep like every child
For I saw you there,
Oh Mother, Mother,
Asleep with a knife in your breast.

Then his father appears and extends his hand.
He scolds him, tall and transparent.
And says: Avram, enter the house at once.
My son, Avram, come home quickly.

And Avram replies:
Oh Father, Father,
There I'm afraid to close my eyes
For I saw you there
Oh Father, Father,
Sleeping still, with no head on your shoulders.

And then his little sister appears
Calling him home, weeping, to bed.
But Avram replies: You are sleeping there.
On your cheeks are the tears of the dead.

Then the seventy nations appear to him
And declare:
We're after you, with seventy warrants and seventy axes
To this house we will get you back!

And lay you down in your bed we will.
Like your father you'll sleep so still!

And Avram in the dream
Cries " Father!"
And " Mother!"and she replies.
I am glad! Were it not for the knife in my breast

My heart would break in two.

Then the night fell silent
The moon grew dim
And the flash of daggers on the hunt
The word of the Lord came to Avram the boy,
Sleeping on the stair:

Saying "Do not fear,
Do not fear, oh Avram
For I shall make thee mighty.
Go forth through the night of dagger and blood
Unto the Land I shall show thee.

"Go forth through the night of dagger and blood
As a beast, as a worm, as a bird.
I will bless those who bless you, Abraham.
And curse those who curse you."

***

And so, this chapter in history
"The refugee problem" was named!
But that's not the problem
My pen-pushing pals
It's not what rips folders or barbed wire
That's not what drives the ships to sea, say I!

They are driven by ancient thunder from on high
They are driven by command of a nation's birth.
By God's word to Avram.

**

And Abraham trembled and fell on his face
And went forth from home and gate
For the command that thundered to Avram the father
Still thunders to Avram the lad.[13]

It is the parent, a mother with a knife in her heart, who bequeaths redemption to her son. God, as the author of the command, is replaced by the vision of national rebirth and independence.[14] A political mandate is phrased in the manner of the divine command: "Go forth through the night of dagger and blood / Unto the land I shall show you." The boy is led from the knife of the Holocaust to Zionist redemption. The command is given by the living-dead against the command of the seventy nations of the world, who are portrayed here as the binders, advising the survivor to go back to his death-bed.

The original edict is reversed by the thunderous command of an historical metaphysical entity, who urges the child Avram to arise from the valley of the dead and go forward to the promised land. The encounter between Abraham and God has been secularized. The child Avram is commanded to fulfill the imperative of destiny—i.e. the goal of national redemption. The roles of the characters have been dramatically reversed. The father does not sacrifice his son; he himself is slaughtered together with his family. The lad is not a passive victim; he is the boy Avram before the covenant was ratified. He is called to rise up like a Phoenix and become the nation that regenerates itself in the land. Thus Avram is both object and subject.

In the intertextual space, the inversion of the symbolic values reflects itself in the changed order of the biblical sequences. Alterman uses midrashic strategy to reverse the order of these sequences as he places chapter 22 וַיֵּרָא ("And the Lord appeared") in Genesis before chapter 12 לֶךְ-לְךָ ("Get thee out"). Thus the section in which God commands Abraham to leave his motherland stands as an ironic analogy to the imperative of destiny that forces the victim of the Holocaust to leave his exile and go forth to the promised land. Moreover, Alterman reveals the latent intratextuality in the biblical text. The command "Get thee out" is echoed in the narrative of the *Aqedah* ("Get thee into the land of Moriah") (Genesis 22:2).[15] In the Bible, it is the revival of the nation consequent upon the covenant with God; here it is the revival of the nation consequent upon the catastrophe. Alterman enhances the historical situation by transforming the biblical text through hyperbole, a process of enhancement of a descriptive term.[16] The collocation "night of knife and blood" is a metaphor that stirs the reader profoundly.

The biblical command "Get thee out" is similarly enhanced. Here the command is "Go forth... /As a beast, as a worm, as a bird: On earth, through the crevices and in the air." The paronomasia between the words רָעַם ("thundered") and the root אמ"ר (in the biblical text וַיֹּאמֶר) conjures up the transformation of God's command into the historical imperative of destiny. These intertextual strategies evoke the numinous elements in the historical moment, highlighting Alterman's eschatological ideology, which links destruction to redemption.

The development from Alterman to Gouri (linked by the "knife in the heart" and the signifier "boy"), from the literature of the yishuv to the Palmach generation, reflects a turning away from exaltation towards resignation. One can trace the ideological and political evolution in modern Hebrew literature through the different meanings given to the sacrifice. For Gouri, the sacrifice is a deterministic given, offering no consolation of future redemption, a result of genetic coding rather than choice. In contrast, for Alterman, it is imbued with vocation–the victim becomes the redeemer.[17] In the early 1950s one encounters signs of transition from collectivism to individualism, from ideological to psychological models in modern Hebrew poetry. Role reversals occur in expressing private existential moments. In the midst of the intensely personal experience of losing one's parents, the offspring see themselves as binders/sacrificers. This interpretation of the parents' vulnerability is ahistorical and will repeat itself throughout the generations. Yehiel Mar, for example, a contemporary of Alterman, rewrites the narrative to explore the feelings of a son who buries his father. In his 'עקידה' father and son climb the mountain together. But whereas the old man stumbles, the younger man, confident in his strength, feels loved even by the landscape. The boy's superior power is implied throughout the poem, which ends with the lines:

אַךְ הַנַּעַר נִגַּשׁ וְשָׁתַק,

עוֹד הָאָב אֶת יָדוֹ לֹא הִשְׁמִיט,

אָז אָמַר

מָה אָמַר לוֹ יִצְחָק

שֶׁאַבְרָם אֶת פָּנָיו הֵלִיט?

The boy steps forward in silence,
And the father does not yet let down his hand.
Then he said –
What did Isaac say to him

To make Abram hide his face?[18]

The reader can only guess: Did the son tell the father that the latter's time had come? Such a farewell to parents reverses the role of the characters in the biblical paradigm. Here it is the old parents who are bound by the threat of imminent death. Thus in many cases, the *Aqedah* sheds national or collective significance and becomes a metaphor for personal trauma–in this case, for being orphaned.

The transition from an ideological model to a psychological one can best be seen in T. Carmi's poetry, which is introspective and based primarily on personal, intimate experience. Carmi dedicated an entire collection of poems to the existential circumstances of the "divorcee." Indeed, the experi-

ence of divorce is central to his poem 'פַּחַד יִצְחָק' ("The Fear of Isaac"), translated here as "The Sacrifice."

אַף־עַל־פִּי שֶׁלֹּא מֵת יִצְחָק מַעֲלֶה עָלָיו הַכָּתוּב כְּאִלּוּ מֵת וְאֶפְרוֹ מוּטָל עַל גַּבֵּי הַמִּזְבֵּחַ
(מִדְרַשׁ הַגָּדוֹל)

הַלַּיְלָה חָלַמְתִּי שֶׁבְּנִי לֹא חָזַר.

הוּא בָּא אֵלַי וְאָמַר לִי:
בִּהְיוֹתִי קָטָן וּבִהְיוֹתָךְ
לֹא רָצִיתָ לְסַפֵּר לִי
אֶת סִפּוּר עֲקֵדַת יִצְחָק,
לְבַעֵת אוֹתִי בְּמַאֲכֶלֶת, אֵשׁ וָאַיִל.

אֲבָל עַכְשָׁו שָׁמַעְתָּ אֶת קוֹלָהּ.
הִיא לָחֲשָׁה, אֲפִלּוּ לֹא צִוְּתָה -
(יָדָהּ מְלֵאָה קוֹלוֹת וְהִיא
דִּבְּרָה אֶל מִצְחֲךָ וְאֶל עֵינֶיךָ:)
כָּךְ?
וּכְבָר מִהַרְתָּ אֶל הַמַּחֲבוֹא,
שָׁלַפְתָּ מַאֲכֶלֶת, אֵשׁ וָאַיִל
וּכְהֶרֶף־עַיִן
אֶת בִּנְךָ, אֶת יְחִידָךְ.

הַלַּיְלָה חָלַמְתִּי שֶׁבְּנִי לֹא חָזַר.
חִכִּיתִי לְשׁוּבוֹ מִבֵּית־הַסֵּפֶר,
וְהוּא הִתְמַהְמַהּ.
וּכְשֶׁסִּפַּרְתִּי לָהּ,
הִיא שָׂמָה אֶת יָדָהּ עָלַי
וְרָאִיתִי אֶת כָּל הַקּוֹלוֹת שֶׁרָאָה.

*Even though Isaac did not die, Scripture refers to him as if he had died and his
ashes had been scattered upon the altar (Midrash Hagadol)*

Last night I dreamt that my son did not return.

He came to me and said:
When I was little and you were,
You would not tell me
The story of the binding of Isaac,
to frighten me with the knife, fire, and ram.

But now you've heard her voice.
She whispered, didn't even command -

(her hand full of voices, and she
said to your forehead and to your eyes:)
is it so?
And already you ran to your hiding-place,
drew out the knife, fire, the ram
And in a flash
your son, your only one.

Last night I dreamt that my son did not return.
I waited for him to come back from school.
and he was late.
And when I told her,
she put her hand upon me,
and I saw all the voices
he had seen.[19]

Here the trial moves from the collective consciousness to the family unit, and the act of divorce is given a surprising twist by the ancient myth. Carmi creates another Midrash based on the interpretation given in the Midrash Hagadol on the question of how it occurred that Isaac did not return with his father, as it is written: "and Abraham returned to his young men." The ominous intertext—midrashic as well as biblical—serves to elevate the personal modern experience and at the same time imbue it with a feeling of imminent awe.

The text shifts between dream and reality; between the biblical sacrifice and sacrifice as a symbol of guilt. Now it is the "other woman" who is the author of the command; in Greimas' terminology she is "the sender." The weight of interpretation shifts onto psychological ground. Sacrifice as a test of faith is translated into parental sacrifice. Sublime biblical episodes echo in the mundane modern experience. "And I saw all the voices/ he had seen" calls to mind the episode of the Israelites who "saw" the voices on Mount Sinai at the giving of the Torah. The irony of comparing the sinful voices of the other woman, absorbed through her hands, with the giving of the Ten Commandments, the pinnacle of morality, enhances the trauma of the man, the father, who is forced by love to betray his son, and lends the text a further numinous dimension.

The syntactically incomplete sentences of the poem, such as "When I was little and you were," likewise remind us of the biblical narrative technique by alluding to the narrative gaps in the original story. In the Bible, however, such gaps are neither in the syntax nor within the sentences; rather, they are between sentences, as demonstrated in Erich Auerbach's

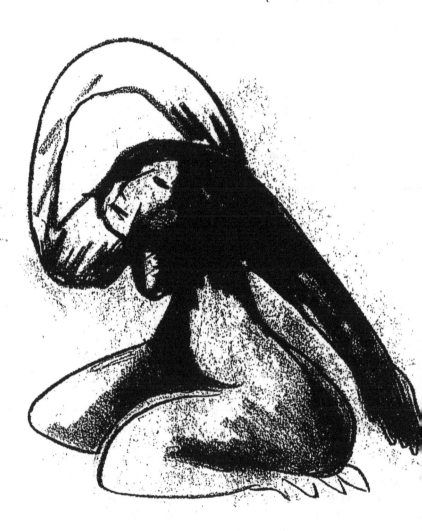

Mimesis, thus leaving the task of exegesis to the reader. By leaving sentences incomplete, the modern poem further taxes the competent reader.

The Hebrew title 'פַּחַד יִצְחָק', literally translated as the "Fear of Isaac," has a long semantic history. In the Book of Genesis (31:42, 53), the Deity is twice referred to as the "Fear of Isaac." Thus the title of the modern poem places it in an intertextual space, and confrontation elevates the father's act and the fear of the "betrayed" son to a loftier yet also more menacing level. The fear of Isaac becomes also the fear of Abraham. There is always, it would seem, a knife-threat lurking in the "hiding place," hovering over the relationship of fathers and sons, as the unconscious also becomes "a sender." One should add that most *Aqedah* poems are fraught with feelings of guilt that are sometimes in the background and at other times move to the foreground, as in Carmi's poem. The collocation the "Fear of Isaac" is a subversive concept from the perspective of the *Aqedah* narrative, for it includes a psychological element missing in the story itself: what Isaac felt during the ordeal. The fear that entered his mind at the time of the *Aqedah* is not mentioned. It is only heard as an echo one generation later in the words of Jacob to Laban: "If the God of my father, the God of Abraham and the fear of Isaac had not been on my side surely now you would have sent me away empty-handed." (Genesis 31:42). The "Fear of Isaac" becomes synonymous with God's name. It does not appear in Isaac's story, only later in Jacob's account—i.e., the *Aqedah* in the biblical narrative is already transmitted from one generation to another—from Isaac to Jacob. It remains a crucial turning point in the conscience of the collective psyche. Moreover, the fact that it has become synonymous with God's name reveals the extreme significance that was attributed to it in Jewish tradition.

Existential interpretations, and the entrance of the unconscious as another character in the drama, signal the change between the 1948 generation and the literary generation of the State, known as דוֹר הַמְּדִינָה. Tuvia Rübner's poem 'קוֹלוֹת' ("Voices") illustrates this development:

אֲנִי הוֹלֵךְ. תָּמִיד אֲנִי הוֹלֵךְ. לְאָן
אֲנִי הוֹלֵךְ? אֵינֶנִּי כָּאן.

מֵאַיִן הָעֵצִים הָאֵלֶּה בְּיָדִי?
הָאֵשׁ הַזֹּאת? אֵינָם שֶׁלִּי. אֵינִי שֶׁלִּי. בִּכְדִי

אֲנִי בְּעִקְבוֹתָיךְ וְלַשָּׁוְא...

אֲנִי יוֹדֵעַ, בְּנִי, אֲנִי הָאָב.

אֲנִי מוֹלִיךְ אוֹתָךְ. שְׁנֵינוּ הוֹלְכִים יַחְדָּו.

אֵינִי יָשֵׁן. אֵינֶנִּי עֵר.

אֲנִי יָשֵׁן. לִבִּי עֵר.

אַיִל אָחוּז בַּצְּלָעוֹת הַשְּׁחוֹרוֹת.

גִּמְגּוּם דּוֹמֵם מִתְאַלֵּם בֵּין פֹּארוֹת
הַזְּמָן הַמִּסְתַּבֵּךְ בְּיוֹמוֹ וְלֵילוֹ...
כֵּן. הִנֵּנִי.

לֹא!

I walk. I always walk: whither
Do I walk? I am not here.

Where does this wood in my hand come from?
This fire? They are not mine. I am not mine. In vain

I walk in your footsteps, for naught...

I know, my son, I am the father.
I lead you. We two go together.

I do not sleep. I am not awake.

I sleep. My heart is awake.

A ram is caught in the black ribcage.

A silent muttering goes mute among the boughs of
Time entangled in its day and night...
Yes. Here am I.

No![20]

We find ourselves in an entirely different atmosphere, a prolonged psychic reality where the binding is internalized without any dramatic event, any relation to history, national destiny or moral commitment. It amounts to a sort of constant existential sleepwalking, lacking either direction or meaning. Although the atmosphere is surrounded by a haze, clear and poignant questions of identity and cognition loom large. Rübner focuses on the only explicit dialogue in the biblical narrative, namely the conversation between Abraham and Isaac on their way to the site of the sacrifice. In "Odysseus Scar" Auerbach says: "The conversation between Abraham and Isaac on the way to the place of sacrifice is only an interruption of the heavy silence, and makes it all the more burdensome."[21] The silence is further underlined by the title "Voices," which are voices of the unconscious. In Rübner's interpretation, the climb is refigured—from actual space into mind space.

Like a stream-of-consciousness narrative, the poem stalls and stutters, expressing an incoherent and curtailed jumble of thoughts. Sometimes incomplete sentences fade into three dots, expressing bewilderment. Although the text incorporates details from the story of the Binding, even those details do not belong to the somnambulist, for he does not belong to himself. This is the negation of the self in the cycle of time. Rübner's text brings out a later perspective—one that is thoroughly existential and that speaks of a human condition in which fate is decreed from within the self.

The modern text deconstructs the patriarchal code, as the question of who is leading whom is blurred. The reader is uncertain if the father leads at all, or whether his actions have any purpose. The logic of causality dissipates itself. For a moment it seems that the father is leading his son: "I lead you." Yet he immediately corrects himself: "We two go together." Ironically, we two go יַחְדָּו ("together") and לַשָּׁוְא ("in vain") rhyme, deconstructing the original unity bonding father and son—signified by the phrase וַיֵּלְכוּ שְׁנֵיהֶם יַחְדָּו—into a meaningless modern existence. Changes of subject abound: the reader does not know who is speaking. Only Isaac could ask: "Where does this wood in my hand come from?" But who is it that asks: "This Fire?" and who says: "Here I am" and who negates these questions?

הנני, a loaded copula in the Hebrew language, reinforces the existential sense of being alive in the poem. In the original narrative, Abraham answers הנני three times: twice vocalized as הִנֵּנִי and once הִנֶּנִּי. The modern poet secularizes the scriptural text by using the modern punctuation הִנְנִי. The second biblical הִנֶּנִּי, in reply to Isaac looking for his father, is somewhat menacing and threatening, dramatically foretelling the imminent sacrifice. The negation in Rübner's poem, the cry "No!"—I am not—is thus all the more powerful. Such a closure is superimposed over the biblical canvas of obedience. The modern text expresses a total refusal.

The constant use of verbs in the present tense accentuates a feeling of stagnation, a hopeless, dead-end situation. The shifts in mood of the speaking subject create a sense of somnambulism, evoked by a phrase from the Song of Songs: "I sleep. My heart is awake." An intertext of love is used here to portray a nightmare. Both father and son are caught in a double bind.

By extension, a sound signifier of life progresses towards deadly silence, towards nothingness. "No!" is the poem's last desperate cry, its final utterance. Even before this point, "A silent muttering goes mute" and becomes entangled in the boughs of time (mirroring the ram's entangled horns in a reversal of signifiers), until complete stillness sets in, a complete negation of being. Here is an individual trapped in a void of meaninglessness. The "I" of the poem is repeated six times at the beginnings of the lines. An individual without his people, without his nation. There is no one to give the command, nor is there an explanation or purpose for such a command. The father's words are not reinforced by the son, as the son cannot understand this futile existence. And if their fate binds them, it only serves to drag them into an abyss. Existential angst hovers over the text.

Reading the poem in the context of the Holocaust raises the theme of the limits of verbal representation in attempting to respond to the recent catastrophe–the poem voices the paralyzing silence that hit the survivors for many years.

A major literary development occurred once the immediate shock of the Holocaust had begun to fade. Only then was the pathos of the founding fathers' poetry, and the still lofty tone of the 1948 generation, replaced by the ironic inflections of the post-State writers. Removed from the collective ideas of Zionism and Judaism, a process of demythologization takes place. The *Aqedah* becomes a legitimate target for a linguistic playfulness that exploits the contemporary development of vernacular Hebrew. Literature moves from ideology to poetics.

As in the dramas using biblical archetypes in the 1960s and 1970s, one of the methods of breaking with norms is the representation of lofty themes in colloquial language. Until the sixties, dialogues in biblical dramas tended to be written in literary language. Such was also the case with poetry. Regarding the role of God, author of the command of sacrifice, there is a gradual transition to the absence of any edict–or at least to an edict characterized by the absurd, indicating the strong influence of existentialism on Hebrew literature of the times.

This displacement can be observed in the poetry of David Avidan, one of the most innovative and prophetic figures among the דּוֹר הַמְּדִינָה ("state generation") poets. Avidan rewrites the *Aqedah* narrative to throw light upon the universal existential condition, rather than to focus on the specific Jewish-Israeli situation. Human existence is viewed here both as a perpetual *Aqedah* and as a perpetual redemption from the *Aqedah*–a concept derived from existentialist philosophy. The most poignant expression of existential angst appears in his eleven-poem cycle "Curriculum Vitae," of which the following is the third poem.[22]

"אִמָּא, אֵינִי רוֹצֶה לָמוּת!"
קָרָא הָאִישׁ בְּקִצֶּהַשְּׁנוֹתָיו.
הָרְאוּת הָיְתָה גְּרוּעָה בְּאוֹתוֹ יוֹם,
וְקוֹל אִמּוֹ נִשְׁלַף אֵלָיו
מִקִּרְבַּתְּיּוֹק, כִּרְשָׁרוּשׁ נְיָר:
"הָיָה לִי פַּעַם בֵּן, בְּנִי,
וְהָיָה לִי פַּעַם רֶחֶם, בְּנִי,
וְהָיָה לָנוּ פַּעַם סִכּוּי, בְּנִי".

"אַבָּא, אֵינִי רוֹצֶה לָמוּת!"
קָרָא הָאִישׁ בְּק צֶהַשְּׁנוֹתָיו.
מֶזֶג־הָאֲוִיר הָיָה בָּהִיר, וְאָבִיו
הִפְרִיחַ בּוּעוֹת אֶל הָאוֹר הַמָּלוּחַ:
"הַמַּלְאָךְ כְּבָר כִּתֵּת אֶת הַמַּאֲכֶלֶת, בְּנִי,
לְכַמָּה וְכַמָּה עִתִּים, בְּנִי,
עַל כַּמָּהוְכַמָּה הָרִים, בְּנִי".

"סַבָּא, אֵינִי רוֹצֶה לָמוּת!"
קָרָא הָאִישׁ בְּקִצֶּהַשְּׁנוּ תָיו.
הַיָּם הָיָה שָׁקוּף וְאַלְגַּלִּי,
וְסָבוֹ שָׁרַק לוֹ מִתּוֹךְ הַצֶּדֶף:
"עַכְשָׁו יֵשׁ לִי שְׁנֵי כַּרְטִיסִים, נֶכְדִּי,
וְעוֹד אוֹמְרִים שֶׁבַּשָּׁנַיִם, נֶכְדִּי,
הַכֹּל נִכְפָּל פִּישְׁנַיִם, נֶכְדִּי".

"קִצֶּה שְׁנוֹתַי, אֵינִי רוֹצֶה לָמוּת!"
קָרָא הָאִישׁ בְּקִצֶּהַשְּׁנוֹתָיו לִקְצֵה
שְׁנוֹתָיו בְּקִצֶּשְׁנוֹתָיו,
אֲבָל אָז עוֹד הָיָה מִקֶּדְּמַדַּי.
"בְּרַח מִמֶּנִּי דֶּרֶךְ הַשָּׁעוֹת",
הִצִּיעַ מַלְאַכְהַמָּוֶת. "לָמַהלְּךָ
לְעָרֵב גוֹרְמִים סוֹתְרִים כָּלְךָ
בְּעִנְיָן אָבוּד כָּלְךָ בְּרֶגַע
נָכוֹן כָּל־כָּךְ?"

"Mom, I don't want to die!"
Cried the man at his endofdays.
Visibility was poor that day,
His mother's voice was pulled
From her innerfile, like rustling paper:
"I had a son once, son,
And I had a womb once, son,

We once had a chance, son."

"Dad, I don't want to die!"
Cried the man at his endofdays.
The weather was clear. His father
Blew bubbles to the salted light:·
"The angel's already beaten his sword, son,
Into several timeshares, son,
On so-and-somany hills, son."

"Grandpa, I don't want to die!"
Cried the man at his endofdays.
The sea was limpid and calm,
His grandfather whistled from a shell:
"I have two tickets now, boy,
And they say that in twos, boy,
Everything doubles in two, boy."

"My endofdays, I don't want to die!"
Cried the man at his endofdays to end
Ofdays at the endofdays,
But it was toosoon.
"Run from me by way of the hours,"
Offered angelofdeath. "Whydoyou
Mix such contradictory elements
In such lost case at sucha
Right moment?"

Existential fright in the face of mortality constitutes the matrix of this cycle.
In the first three poems the reader encounters a speaker at different stages
of his life. During each stage, his attitude to death is different. In every
poem, the speaker turns to external, almost abstract entities that point either
to his past (mother, father, grandfather) or to his future (children, grandchil-
dren). All of the figures answer him in their own language, rejecting his
attempts to find meaning in life by following their patterns of experience.

Although the links between the cycle of poems and the biblical paradigm
seem weak, on careful rereading the main textual elements–the crifice,
the hills, the sword/knife, the angel–become evident traces of the intertext,
enough to evoke intertextual speculation. In the first poem, the speaker
wants to die when he is in "the midst of his years." But when he turns to
his father, the latter answers him: "The angel has already confiscated the
knife, son / and I know of no better gallows than it, son." Because in the

modern context martyrdom is devoid of religious, national, or even psychological meaning, man can no longer turn to "the Sacrifice" as a meaningful type of death. This is not an option, just as the mother cannot take her son "back" into her old womb. Similarly, the grandfather relates that he himself has "only a one-way ticket"—that is, each person is responsible for himself and his choices and cannot tie his life's journey to that of another. Finally the speaker turns to "the midst of his days"—that is, to his own existence, but the Angel of Death declares that he must "march to him through the years," neither pleading for an untimely death nor turning to others for help. The knowledge of death compels man to continue living and demands that he extract "every moment in so beautiful an evening."

In *Curriculum Vitae et Mortis* we find the speaker "at the end of days." Close to the darker side of the spectrum, he no longer wants to die. He turns to his father, who answers him: "The angel's already beaten his sword, son, / Into several timeshares, son, / On so-and-so many hills, son." The *Aqedah*, i.e. consciousness of death, is a universal existential predicament. Finally, death suggests that he flee from him "through the hours"—in other words, exploit every moment of his existence. Every moment is the right moment to live or die.

Avidan has made a thoroughly Sartrean, existential statement. God does not exist, and death is the author of the command to die. The biblical angel is replaced by an angel of death who, as in Kafka's *The Trial*, advises the speaker "at the end of days" not "to mix up contradictory factors," for it is a lost cause. What remains to be done? A man must make the most of the hours placed at his disposal, for it is still too soon to plead with death, and it would certainly do no good to call on others for help. In other words, private existence is simultaneously both *Aqedah* and redemption from *Aqedah*: fear of death serves "as the correct moment" for the full sensation of existence. In Sartrean terms, being exists for itself in itself. Man in himself is free and responsible for his own existence. The past is denied, but the freedom of being that is thus attained comes at the price of recognizing the nausea and terror of existential angst itself. The absurd, which, Kierkegaard claims, underlies the biblical text, here becomes an existential absurd.[23]

Avidan's notion of the biblical trial, as detached from national, historical, and religious contexts, becomes a means of portraying human existence: the way we influence our destiny through the choices we make daily (like the choice made by Abraham). Moreover, we have to understand that we are "bound" to this existence, and we cannot shake off our responsibilities to it. Avidan's concept of choice echoes Kierkegaarian philosophy, according to which a human being cannot be an authentic personality when he

significantly limits his responsibility or attempts to escape. Avidan dramatizes a major transformation of the *acteurs* and their roles. It is no longer God
who commands, but our own existence. When we recognize this edict and
the inevitability of death, we have to respond הנני. But simultaneously we
must protest loudly by exploiting each moment to its full extent, thus re-
deeming ourselves from the *Aqedah*.

The signifying force of the existential Angel of Death is enhanced against
the background of Christian resurrection. Shalom Spiegel notes how in the
Midrash, and, even more so, in Christianity, Satan is identified with the
Angel of Death.[24] In Christianity, the victory over Satan is the victory over
death–through the resurrection. By virtue of that victory, believers are
promised new life. Such intertextual space opens up the poem to further
ironic levels of interpretation.

The Victim and The Bound

We now turn to the other dramatis personae of the *Aqedah* narrative: the
binder, the bound, and the victim. The replacement of Isaac by a ram en-
gaged the minds of the liturgical poets long ago, as well as various commen-
tators in the Hebrew tradition. Responding to pogroms, they posed two
questions: Why was that archetypal surrogate not provided again? and Why
is the Jew repeatedly the victim of violence and massacres? Reverberations
of this protest are felt in twentieth-century Hebrew poetry throughout its
collective, idealistic phase, echoing with pathos. In 'עֲקֵידוֹת' ("Bindings"),
Zalman Schneor writes:

וּמַלְאָךְ לֹא נִגְלָה, לְהָשִׁיב יַד שׁוֹחֲטָיו אָחוֹר,
וְאַיִל לֹא נֶאֱחַז בְּקַרְנָיו בַּסְּבָךְ.

The angel did not appear, to hold back the hand of the slaughterers
And the ram was not caught by the horns in the thicket.[25]

The modern poet tends to give voice to the taciturn or mute characters in
the biblical narrative or to those who are absent. Sarah, the main protagonist of the annunciation story, disappears completely when the child she has
borne is about to be sacrificed. Benjamin Galai, a contemporary of Gouri,
is one of the few poets receptive to the feminist point of view. In his interpretation of the narrative, the only person who dies as a result of this trial
is the mother, who is absent. Galai exploits the biblical paradox in the title
of the section that relates her death, which is called 'חַיֵּי שָׂרָה' ("The Life of
Sarah").

וַיִּהְיוּ
חַיֵּי שָׂרָה
מֵאָה שָׁנָה, עֶשְׂרִים שָׁנָה, שֶׁבַע שָׁנִים.

וַתָּמָת -
הִיא נִסְתַּלְּקָה מִן הָעוֹלָם בְּהַר חֶבְרוֹן,
לְקוֹל טְפִיפַת רַגְלֵי הַמְשָׁרְתִים,
שֶׁשָּׁכְחָה אֲפִלּוּ אֶת שְׁמוֹתָם.
כָּל יְדִידֵי הַמִּשְׁפָּחָה לִוּוּ, כִּתְּפוּ אֶת אֲרוֹנָהּ,
לִמְקוֹם מְנוּחָתוֹ הָאַחֲרוֹן.
קְרָשָׁיו, נָמְלָה שָׁם הַבָּרָה, הָיוּ דַקִּים־מִן־הַדַּקִּים,
קַלִּים־קַלִּים.

וַיִּהְיוּ
חַיֵּי שָׂרָה
מֵאָה שָׁנָה, עֶשְׂרִים שָׁנָה, שֶׁבַע שָׁנִים.
שְׁנֵי חַיֵּי שָׂרָה.

וַתָּמָת -
אַךְ בֶּאֱמֶת כָּבָה נֵרָהּ יָמִים רַבִּים, רַבִּים לִפְנֵי
שֶׁמִּשְׁכָּנָהּ הָאַחֲרוֹן הָיָה עָפָר.
וְהָאָרוֹן שֶׁבּוֹ שָׁכְבָה הָיָה עָשׂוּי כָּל־הַשָּׁנִים
זִכְרוֹן עֵצִים מְבֻקָּעִים עַל הַר אַחֵר,
עַל הַר אַחֵר, בְּאֶרֶץ מוֹרִיָּה.

And the life of Sarah
was
a hundred years, twenty years, seven years.

And she died
She departed from the world in Mount Hebron.
To the pattering of the feet of servants
Whose names she even forgot.
All the friends of the family came to the funeral.
Shouldered her coffin.
To its last place of rest.
Its planks, it was said, were the thinnest of thin
The lightest of light.

And the life of Sarah
was
A hundred years, twenty years, seven years.
The years of Sarah's life.

And she died –
But really,
Her candle had gone out many days, many before
Her last resting place was dust.
And the coffin she lay in was made of all the years,
The memory of wood cleft on another mount,
On another mount, in the Land of Moriah.[26]

For Galai, Sarah becomes every mother whose son has been exposed to mortal danger. Indeed, even Rashi's commentary discusses the contiguity between the trial and Sarah's death, to which he brings a literary interpretation: "The death of Sarah follows the binding of Isaac because by it, when her son seemed destined to be slaughtered, indeed was almost slaughtered, her soul 'flew away' [פָּרְחָה נִשְׁמָתָהּ] from her and she died."

Galai exploits the multi-temporal coatings of modern Hebrew, investing them with poetic and ideological meanings. Typical of first generation native-born Israeli poets, he is acutely aware of his generation's position in Jewish history and of Hebrew's palimpsestic character.[27] The linguistic transitions here are calculated and brusque, so that the poem passes from the biblical to the mishnaic register, and then on to contemporary speech. The extreme difficulty of translating into English these natural and unforced transitions from one register to another only serves to emphasize the exceptional synchronic nature of Hebrew.

The second stanza begins with a biblical quotation, וַתָּמָת שָׂרָה ("and Sarah died"), followed immediately by a mishnaic collocation, הִיא נִסְתַּלְּקָה ("she departed"), which seems, so to speak, to "translate" the biblical word וַתָּמָת. Suddenly modernity erupts in the shape of a typical line from an Israeli newspaper, employing an idiom from Israeli army life: כֻּתְּפוּ, translated here as "shouldered," that evokes the image of a contemporary army funeral, where the true victim is the mother, not the son.[28] The sharp linguistic tra.. sitions function to conjure up Sarah as a universal historical figure who dies of a catastrophe conceived in her imagination only. Further, with the phrase שְׁנֵי חַיֵּי ("two lives"),[29] Galai exploits intratextuality in separate Genesis narratives dealing with two respective parents—Sarah (Gen. 23:1) and Jacob (Gen. 47:9), both of whom almost lost their offspring. Revealing the links between the two intertexts, the poem leads the reader to form one conclusion: near bereavement can be as fatal as bereavement. In Galai's interpretation of the *Aqedah*, then, all the other characters have vanished. His is a story about the loneliness of the mother. For the modern sensibility, she is the sole victim.

In order to assess the ideological and political developments in Hebrew poetry, we now turn to the stage in the rewriting of the *Aqedah* where the ram replaces the intended sacrifice. 'הַגִּבּוֹר הָאֲמִתִּי שֶׁל הָעֲקֵדָה' ("The Real Hero of The Sacrifice") by Yehuda Amichai exemplifies the trend of the seventies and eighties towards demythicizing national and social myths and archetypes in Israeli poetry.

הַגִּבּוֹר הָאֲמִתִּי שֶׁל הָעֲקֵדָה הָיָה הָאַיִל
שֶׁלֹּא יָדַע עַל הַקְּנוּנְיָה בֵּין הָאֲחֵרִים.
הוּא כְּמוֹ הִתְנַדֵּב לָמוּת בִּמְקוֹם יִצְחָק.
אֲנִי רוֹצֶה לָשִׁיר עָלָיו שִׁיר זִכָּרוֹן,
עַל הַצֶּמֶר הַמִּתְלַתֵּל וְעַל עֵינָיו הָאֱנוֹשִׁיּוֹת
עַל הַקַּרְנַיִם שֶׁהָיוּ שְׁקֵטוֹת כָּל כָּךְ בְּרֹאשׁוֹ הֶחָי
וְאַחַר שֶׁנִּשְׁחַט עָשׂוּ מֵהֶן שׁוֹפָרוֹת
לְקוֹל תְּרוּעַת מִלְחַמְתָּם
אוֹ לְקוֹל תְּרוּעַת שִׂמְחָתָם הַגַּסָּה.

אֲנִי רוֹצֶה לִזְכֹּר אֶת הַתְּמוּנָה הָאַחֲרוֹנָה
כְּמוֹ תַּצְלוּם יָפֶה בְּעִתּוֹן אָפְנָה מְעֻדָּן:
הַצָּעִיר הַשָּׁזוּף וְהַמְפֻנָּק בְּבִגְדָיו הַמְגֻנְדָּרִים
וּלְיָדוֹ הַמַּלְאָךְ הַלָּבוּשׁ שִׂמְלַת מֶשִׁי אֲרֻכָּה
לְקַבָּלַת פָּנִים חֲגִיגִית.
וּשְׁנֵיהֶם בְּעֵינַיִם רֵיקוֹת
מַבִּיטִים אֶל שְׁנֵי מְקוֹמוֹת רֵיקִים

וּמֵאֲחוֹרֵיהֶם, כְּרֶקַע צִבְעוֹנִי, הָאַיִל
נֶאֱחָז בַּסְּבַךְ בְּטֶרֶם שְׁחִיטָה.
וְהַסְּבַךְ יְדִידוֹ הָאַחֲרוֹן.

הַמַּלְאָךְ הָלַךְ הַבַּיְתָה
יִצְחָק הָלַךְ הַבַּיְתָה
וְאַבְרָהָם וֵאלֹהִים הָלְכוּ מִזְּמָן.

אֲבָל הַגִּבּוֹר הָאֲמִתִּי שֶׁל הָעֲקֵדָה
הוּא הָאַיִל.

The real hero of the sacrifice was the ram
Who had no idea about the conspiracy of the others.
He apparently volunteered to die in place of Isaac.
I want to sing a memorial song about the ram,
His curly wool and human eyes,
The horns, so calm in his living head.
When he was slaughtered, they made *shofars* of them,

To sound the blast for their war
Or the blast of their coarse joy.

I want to remember the last picture
Like a beautiful photo in an exquisite fashion magazine:
The tanned, spoiled youngster all spiffed up,
And beside him the angel, clad in a long silk gown
For a formal reception.
Both with hollow eyes
Observe two hollow places,

And behind them, as a colored background, the ram
Grasping the thicket before the slaughter.
And the thicket was his last friend.

The angel went home
Isaac went home
And Abraham and God left much earlier.

But the real hero of the sacrifice
Is the ram.[30]

In a reversal typical of the provocative poetry of the eighties and nineties, Amichai, the "anti-political political poet,"[31] transforms the eloquent silence and loneliness hovering over the biblical narrative into a noisy social ritual. He voices disdain both for the glorification of sacrifice and for the romanticism of death that characterized the literature of the yishuv. Challenging the self-righteous attitude towards victimization in Israeli culture, the poet of love and of war against war, who praises the quotidian values of simply living and loving and who wants to die in his own bed, identifies the innocent anonymous soldier as the "real" victim, while "the other people" represent the political establishment. Distancing and defining himself vis-à-vis that establishment, he completely demythicizes the biblical myth by ridiculing the social rituals typically associated with war victims. He does so through a process of estrangement, for who has ever paid attention to the innocent mute ram, the surrogate victim for Isaac, as a subject in itself?

The deflation of the lofty paradigm is also enacted through a latent paronomasia. The biblical root רא"ה in the poem generates the image of a photo, ironically alluding to the increased number of memorial photograph albums in Israeli society, subsequent to each war. Thus Amichai empties the ancient root of all the cognitive and psychological implications ascribed to it by previous generations, and lends it a quotidian meaning.

Seen from the perspective of a detached secular reader, Isaac is a spoiled brat "all spiffed up." The story is just deception and delusion, for the ram is the true victim. This interpretation stems from Amichai's attitude to the Scriptures. Unlike many of his contemporaries, his is a complete secular biblicism, one that does not teem with the tensions between the mundane and the transcendental as in the poetry of Amir Gilboa, Nathan Zach, or Dalia Rabikovitch.

Everything is trivialized in the contrast between the lofty biblical subject and its depiction in a colloquial linguistic register. Everyday language, bordering on slang, effects the transition from transcendental height to a human existential environment that rejects any links with tradition and cultural heritage. Notice the implied renunciation of social ritual in the line: "To sound the blast for their war/ Or the blast of their coarse joy." After all, the ram's horns become the shofars for the fanfare. And it is the ram that is portrayed here in the most lyrical manner ("the curly wool and human eyes").[32] Above all, Amichai's sad playfulness is evident here, as he claims that the story is not merely fiction, but that from the very start everyone knew it to be a fake.

This perception marks a turning point in the evolution of Hebrew poetry. Amichai retells the biblical story, adding elements that were never in the original, thus rupturing the chain of causality so essential to the narrative. Previously, poets were faithful to the Aristotelian principle that the author of a tragedy could use myth with limited freedom, as long as he did not challenge his audience's conception of the myth. Poets opened up the text, but did not alter its basic structure. Amichai, however, contradicts and violates the causal scriptural structure underlying the narrative. The entire story is recast in the mode of new poetic conventions: the narrator steps into the fiction in order to sing a poem to the ram's memory, thereby undermining the authority of the omniscient narrator of the original story.

Through a provocative rereading of the biblical paradigm, Amichai attempts to understand the infrastructure of a cultural model. In every *Aqedah* there is a ram. The decision as to who is the victim is a political and ideological one.

A meta-poetic interpretation is exemplified in David Avidan's parody of the Christian vision of the Binding of Isaac. The Church fathers believed that the *Aqedah* prefigured the Crucifixion. Avidan mocks this interpretation. In his 'טְיוּטָה' ("Draft"), such a typological perspective produces only a new literary Judeo-Christian Bacchanalia.

דָּוִד עוֹקֵד אֶת מָשִׁיחַ
וּמְעַכֵּב אֶת הַגְּאוּלָה.

עֲקֵדַת יִצְחָק
פְּעֻלַּת־הַסָּחָה,
הַצָּתָה מְקֻדֶּמֶת.

הַצְּלִיבָה
חֲזָרָה־כְּלָלִית,
הַצָּתָה מְאֻחֶרֶת,
עִבּוּד לְמַחֲזֶמֶר

יֵשׁוּ כָּפִיל־עֶלְיוֹן.

David binds the messiah
And delays redemption.

The binding of Isaac
a diversionary action,
an early ignition.

The Crucifixion,
a dress rehearsal
late ignition.
musical version.

Jesus super-double.[33]

The notion of intertextuality for Avidan is a part of the recycling of culture;
a culture made of duplications and copies. The poet-jester David portrays
the *Aqedah*, together with the Crucifixion, as a dress rehearsal for the musical *Jesus Christ Superstar* (the irony is accentuated, since Avidan has always
claimed that he writes only one draft of a poem—חַד־טִיוּטָאִי). "Draft" relates
to the ongoing function of the *Aqedah* myth in western culture. The motif of
a fresh "draft"—the rewriting and reshaping of myths that function as
meta-narratives in western culture—repeats itself throughout the poem,
starting with its title and continuing through theatrical images. The lack of
telos in the tale, and the multiplicity of its occurrences within western culture, transform it into an absurdity. Avidan, one of the forerunners of
postmodernism in Hebrew literature, evokes the postmodernist notion of a
copy of a copy without an original source. Even the biblical source is deflated, since at the furthest limit of its duplication it is changed into a
noncanonic genre—a stage musical.

Avidan addresses the palimpsestic nature of culture through his multi-

layered diction, which combines ancient and modern registers, using jour-
nalese, army slang, and colloquialisms. However, since "the purpose of battle is dialogue," as he wrote, he uses intertextuality not only to express his
perspective on a recycled world, but also to create new and original texts.
Thus, the narrative of the Binding becomes a legitimate target for play,
parody, and meta-poetic reflections. A bathetic effect is created through
marked contrast between the registers of spoken Hebrew (army slang, psychological jargon, and contemporary musicals) and the lofty canonical
intertext. Both Amichai and Avidan provocatively trivialize the mythic and
historical associations by reducing the grandiloquent biblical registers to
mundane spoken language. Both poets present the deeply serious side of
the carnivalesque challenge to official linguistic codes.

Intrinsic to the representations of the *Aqedah* in Israeli poetry is the deep
structure of a Janus face, turning simultaneously towards father and son, as
each places the other upon the altar. The son, who emigrates to the Land
of Israel, abandons the father, who is later murdered in the Holocaust; and
the father, who emigrates to Israel, later has a son, only to sacrifice him on
the altar of national independence. It is as though the *Aqedah* were a kind
of heritage passed on from father to son, as in Gouri's 'יְרוּשָׁה', which the son,
in turn, passes on to the father. The same pattern is followed in Amir
Gilboa's 'יִצְחָק', written in response to the loss of his family in the Holocaust,
where binder and victim are switched in the nightmare of the child.

לִפְנוֹת בֹּקֶר טִיְּלָה שֶׁמֶשׁ בְּתוֹךְ הַיַּעַר
יַחַד עִמִּי וְעִם אַבָּא
וִימִינִי בִּשְׂמֹאלוֹ.

כְּבָרָק לָהֲבָה מַאֲכֶלֶת בֵּין הָעֵצִים.
וַאֲנִי יָרֵא כָּל־כָּךְ אֶת פַּחַד עֵינַי מוּל דָּם עַל הֶעָלִים.

אַבָּא אַבָּא מַהֵר וְהַצִּילָה אֶת יִצְחָק
וְלֹא יֶחְסַר אִישׁ בִּסְעֻדַּת הַצָּהֳרַיִם.

זֶה אֲנִי הַנִּשְׁחָט, בְּנִי,
וּכְבָר דָּמִי עַל הֶעָלִים.
וְאַבָּא נִסְתַּם קוֹלוֹ.
וּפָנָיו חִוְרִים.

וְרָצִיתִי לִצְעֹק, מְפַרְפֵּר לֹא לְהַאֲמִין
וְקוֹרֵעַ הָעֵינַיִם.
וְנִתְעוֹרַרְתִּי.
וְאָזְלַת־דָּם הָיְתָה יַד יָמִין

At dawn, the sun strolled in the forest
together with me and father, and my
right hand was in his left.

Like lightning a knife flashed among
the trees. And I am so afraid of my
eyes' terror, faced by blood on the leaves.

Father, father, quickly save Isaac so
that no one will be missing at the
midday meal.

It is I who am being slaughtered, my son
and already my blood is on the leaves.
And father's voice was
smothered and his face was pale.

And I wanted to scream, writhing not
to believe, and tearing open my eyes.
And I woke up.

And my right hand was drained of
blood.[34]

Like Carmi's 'פַּחַד יִצְחָק', *Yitzhak* might be categorized as a "dream poem,"
a common genre in the literature of the *Aqedah*; a projection between fan-
tasy and reality, between the biblical narrative and the memory of the Holocaust. The victim is now the father, and the boy's childish fear is transformed into guilt feelings towards the parent he has abandoned. The Holocaust has reversed the roles in the nightmare of the Binding, turning the
lyrical self into a modern Isaac whose father is bound and slaughtered. The
emphasis shifts from the collective phase, in both Alterman's and Gouri's
poetry, to the family unit. Neither a trial of faith nor of historical destiny,
this is simply the slaughter of a father in the Holocaust. Now the *Aqedah*
archetype displays a Janus face, which continually changes roles: the binder
becomes the bound, and vice versa. In an historical context, the text reflects
the guilt feelings of the yishuv in Palestine, powerless to rescue the European fathers in the Holocaust.

Gilboa's poem ostensibly opens with an idyllic pastoral scene, narrated
in the voice of the child. The son strolls with his father through a seemingly
sunlit forest. The biblical Mount Moriah has been changed into a European
forest, prefiguring the catastrophe. The speaker, in child-like fashion, first
refers to himself and then to his father ("with me and father"). The sun's

personification, as though it too were a family member gaily accompanying "me and father," establishes the illusion of a child reminiscing innocently about an ordinary outing. The paratactic syntax also serves to evoke a melange of children's speech and biblical language. The idyllic depiction of a father walking hand in hand with his son calls to mind the biblical narrative, where it is said that Abraham and Isaac "went both of them together." In the modern text the intimate bond between father and son is highlighted by the child-like remark that "my right hand was in his left." The intertextual reference to the Song of Songs conjures up the intimate nature of the close bond, which echoes through the poem ("His left hand is under my head and his right hand doth embrace me" [Song of Songs" 2:6]). Love and death are intertwined, as in many other *Aqedah* poems.

In the second stanza, the serene walk is metamorphosed into a nightmarish spectacle. Isaac dramatically foresees the ghastly events that are to be enacted in the verdant forest. Through terror-stricken, wide-open eyes, he visualizes the blood-spattered leaves, even before his own blood and that of his father has been spilt. The fear-laden atmosphere becomes heavy with surreal and grotesque images, reminiscent of a Dali painting. The son gazes with detachment as his hands are being drained of blood, and he wakes, powerless in the face of this horrendous cataclysm. Gilboa's metonymic language differs markedly from that of Alterman and Shlonsky, which tends to be more metaphoric. Even his paratactic syntax, essentially syntagmatic, is characteristic of metonymic language. In 'יִצְחָק', terror is not presented as an internal condition, but is sensuously related to specific physical organs that register external images—for example, the eyes fearful of their own terror, or the limp hands witnessing their own helplessness, powerless in the face of the evil enacted.

The Hebrew reader has no difficulty understanding the narrative of the poem: a father and son stroll through pastoral forest. But the line: "So that no one will be missing in the midday meal" raises a problem. What is a meal doing in this chilling narrative? Hidden and intricate links may surface, particularly in the mind of the Hebrew reader, through an association between the ancient biblical word מַאֲכֶלֶת ("knife"), automatically tied to the biblical *Aqedah*, and the basic common root אכ"ל, relating to food and eating The links are made in a subtle and complex manner; although the root is not specifically mentioned, it is evoked by the word סְעָדָה ("meal"). The Hebrew reader, sometimes subconsciously, identifies the root since lexical decisions in Hebrew are based upon abstract linguistic representations that constitute the root.[35] This paronomasia, like others, engages the reader in a speculative activity, not necessarily in relation to the historical source of the figure, but rather to its signifying force, which has its genesis in the moment of reading. In יִצְחָק' a link is being created between the root and a pictorial mental image. Paronomasia here is based on the image, rather than on links between the roots. (A similar process, mentioned above, appears in Amichai's poem, where a link with the root רא"ה generates a pictorial image of the photograph).

Indeed, the meaning of a Gilboa poem emerges as much from the paronomasia and unusual word relation as directly from the ideas and images. Again in the fourth stanza, we find an example of paronomasia in the image "father's voice was smothered (Hebrew: shut)." In Hebrew, the metaphor applied to the smothered voice (קוֹלוֹ נִסְתָּם) is linked to the colloquial "shut your mouth" or "shut your trap" (the English word "trap" is only borrowed here to suggest the image of a hole in the ground); the same Hebrew word for "shut" is used to describe the final act of covering a person's grave with dust: לִסְתּוֹם אֶת הַגּוֹלֵל.[36]

Gilboa, who deploys various linguistic metaphors in this poem, transforms also the biblical expression פַּחַד יִצְחָק ("Isaac's Fear"). In the traditional sources, the term is a synonym for the Deity (as previously mentioned in the context of T. Carmi's 'פַּחַד יִצְחָק'). Here the expression is reversed to פַּחַד עֵינַי ("my eye's fear (terror)." Indeed, Gilboa's poem brilliantly utilizes the different categories of paronomasia latent in modern Hebrew poetry. Abraham's enigmatic reply to Isaac, אֱלֹהִים יִרְאֶה־לּוֹ הַשֶּׂה לְעֹלָה ("God will provide himself a lamb for a burnt offering") (Gen. 22:9) is inverted to become the terrified cry: וַאֲנִי יָרֵא כָּל כַּךְ אֶת פַּחַד עֵינַי מוּל דָּם עַל הֶעָלִים ("and I am so afraid of my eyes' terror laced by blood on the leaves"). The sound is held in the memory—יָרֵא and יִרְאֶה, yet both the different root and orthography have now turned the meaning upside down. The substitution/inversion of the verb רא"ה signifies not only the transition from the collective to the personal, but the secularization of the archetypal trial. Through this intertextual transformation, a world is established where the Deity is absent. Moreover, the very deconstruction of the sacred collocation פַּחַד יִצְחָק, which in Jewish tradition indicates the taboo on God's name, is an abuse as well as a polemical gesture.

The root רא"ה generates other narratives within the poem. For example, when Isaac wakes מְפַרְפֵּר ("writhing"), which in Hebrew describes a condition between life and death, he violently tears his eyes open (כְּקוֹרֵעַ עֵינַיִם) to escape the nightmare, yet sees instead the reality of a living hell. In Jeremiah 4:30, the same verb appears: תִקְרְעִי בַפּוּךְ עֵינַיִךְ: literally, "you tear at your eyes," but the underlying meaning is to rent the face in painting—i.e., put on make-up (kohl) in order to emphasize the eyes, hoping thus to win grace and salvation at the hour of killing, death, and mourning. In this instance, the painting is in vain, for Zion is not saved.

In Jewish ritual, a tear in the clothes is the poignant signifier of desolation and mourning at funerals. Isaac tears his eyes open to face catastrophe. Hence yet another complex paronomasia is built upon the root רא"ה, and a sign of faith becomes a marker of destruction. In Gilboa's poetry dreams reveal memory. To awaken from a dream ordinarily means to forget. Here the narrator awakens to face the nightmare.

Indeed, 'יִצְחָק' regresses from the intimacy of the opening scene to a devastating reality of destruction and nothingness. The poem is gradually drained of sound and of life; like the hand: "And my right hand was drained of blood." The repetition of the image of the "right hand" closes the cycle of the poem by mirroring the personal "right hand" (יְמִינִי) of the first stanza. However, Gilboa does not write "my right hand," but "[the] right hand," and if that hand is not Isaac's, a further interpretative possibility is inherent in the passage. "The right hand of God" appears in the traditional sources as the hand that defeats the enemies of the Jewish people. In Hebrew, the expression "a drained hand" denotes impotence, an inability to act, playing on the idiom אָזְלַת יָד ("powerlessness"). This collocation implies that the son also becomes a victim, an interpretation that seems to be supported by the proximity of 'יִצְחָק' to the poem 'וְאָחִי שׁוֹתֵק' ("And my Brother is Silent") in Gilboa's volume כְּחֻלִּים וַאֲדֻמִּים ("Blues and Reds"). By breaking up the Hebrew idiom אָזְלַת יָד and turning it into the new linguistic metaphor אָזְלַת דָּם הָיְתָה יַד יָמִין, Gilboa's concrete image not only suggests creeping death. It also reinforces a polemical subtext: that ours is a world without Divine Providence—or worse, a world where the Deity is impotent.

One of the most poignant expressions of ideological and political role reversals appears in the work of Hanoch Levin, the most influential modernist dramatist active in Israel today. Influenced by the Theatre of the Absurd and Artaud's "Theatre of Cruelty," Levin's work is characterized by grotesque scenarios and infused with social criticism.

After the Six Day War, amidst the euphoria consequent upon the unexpected victory with its concomitant glorification of the army, Levin dared to criticize Israel's new sacred cows in his satirical dramas. In his *Queen of The Bath*, a musical review that incorporates poems and sketches, the overarching metaphor for Israel's new situation is a filthy bath in which everyone bathes. First staged in the Chamber Theatre in Tel Aviv in 1970, the play shocked Israeli audiences and even resulted in the censorship of certain provocative passages.

One of the central sketches in the play is called 'עֲקֵדָה', and features a dialogue between Abraham and Isaac. Isaac pleads with his father to slaughter him without hesitation. The dialogue develops into a confrontation between father and son as they exchange roles. Each one alternately plays the victim. As the sketch progresses, the characters becomes increasingly violent and verbally abusive. Finally a heavenly voice is heard, and Isaac is not slaughtered. The words of Abraham at the conclusion clear the way for crucial questions: "What will happen, I wonder, if other fathers have to slaughter their sons? Who will save them?" By depicting Abraham as a senile old man who sets out to execute an arbitrary command without a second thought, Levin presents a modern *Aqedah* devoid of either ethical dimensions or the dilemmas precipitated by parental love.

At a certain stage Abraham announces that he is a victim, a reversal that can also be found in other representative contemporary works. The saving of Isaac similarly undergoes a transformation as the angel and the ram disappear, apparently leaving the deliverance of Isaac to chance since it is not at all clear to whom the mysterious voice that calls out belongs. Through the deautomatization of cliches (Abraham: "One has to slaughter: there is no choice"), Levin simultaneously attacks such sacred cows as the "war without choice" and the State's institutionalization of bereavement. He also directs his arrows at the literature of the 1948 War of Liberation where, for example, in Yigal Mossinsohn's play *In the Negev Plains,* a father sends his son Gidon to battle, knowing full well that he will not return.

Stylistic pathos gradually gives way to rudeness and abuse. The semantic field is layered with slaughter as its main metaphor. Levin manhandles language, exploring the relationship between sacrifice and violence (a theme portrayed brilliantly by Rene Girard in *Violence and The Sacred*).[37]

The poem 'אָבִי היקר, כשתעמוד על קברי' ("Dear father, when you stand over my grave") immediately follows the sketch. It differs in atmosphere, radiating a softer tone. Yet its ideological message is similar. The poem is a monologue of the dead Isaac, who takes his father to task as he is being buried.

אָבִי היקר, כשתעמוד על קברי

אָבִי היקר, כשתעמוד על קברי
זקן ועייף ומאוד עֲרירי,
ותראה איך טומנים את גופי בעפר
ואתה עומד מעלי, אבי,

אל תעמוד אז גאה כל־כך,
ואל תזקוף את ראשך, אבי,

נשארנו עכשיו בשר מול בשר
וזהו הזמן לבכות, אבי.

אז תן לעיניך לבכות על עיני,
ואל תחריש למען כבודי,
דבר־מה שהיה חשוב מכבוד
מוטל עכשיו לרגליך, אבי,

ואל תאמר שהקרבת קורבן,
כי מי שהקריב הייתי אני,
ואל תדבר עוד מלים גבוהות
כי אני כבר מאוד נמוך, אבי.

אבי היקר, כשתעמוד על קברי
זקן ועייף ומאוד ערירי,
ותראה איך טומנים את גופי בעפר -
בקש אז ממני סליחה, אבי.

Dear father, when you stand over my grave
Tired and old and very solitary
And you see how my body is put in the dust,
And you stand above me, father.

Don't stand there then so very proud,
And don't lift your head high, father,
We are left now flesh against flesh
And now is the time to cry, father.

So let your eyes cry on my eyes,
And don't keep silent for my honor's sake.
Something that was more important than honor
Now lies at your feet, father.

And don't say that you made a sacrifice,
For the one sacrificed was me,
And don't say any more high sounding words,
For I am now very low, father.

My dear father, when you stand over my grave
Tired and old and very solitary
And you see how my body is put in the dust,
Ask then my forgiveness.[38]

Levin signals the change from the ethos of siege and vindication experienced by earlier generations to an ethos of guilt and shame. Like Amichai,

he also tries to seize upon something beyond the verbal screen of the myth. For Levin, this is the idea of mourning. He challenges established interpretations of the *Aqedah*, as well as those in early Israeli literature. Abraham is emphatically neither a hero nor a victim. The Kirkegaardian "knight of faith" turns out to be the knight of false honor. The story is seen through the eyes of the dead Isaac. All heroics have been removed, and the retelling of the myth is determined by a fresh ideological perspective. Levin attempts to shake off the pathos and portray a common human situation of death and burial. The son protests against his own potential death; and as the myth vanishes into thin air, what remains is father and son, flesh to flesh.[39]

Soon after the Six Days War שְׁדֵמוֹת, a journal of the kibbutz movement, published a symposium on the subject entitled "The Binding of Isaac and Our Contemporaries." Eli Elon, one of the participants, states:

> If we are honest with ourselves, we have to evaluate our lives and the lives of our friends from the point of view of the dead Isaac, from the point of view of the dead. Then we'll be surprised to discover that many of the slogans and values that seem necessary to us, in order "to give meaning to our lives," and for which we were ready to die, will suddenly seem to us vanity and folly.... Facing the great darkness, what little seems really necessary, what is worth more than a little light of the sun? Maybe if we understood this we would be less willing to sacrifice our lives and take the lives of other people in the name of false, inflated values.[40]

Indeed, the generation of the Six Day War called themselves דּוֹר יִצְחָק (" the generation of Isaac") ("That name," Gouri once told me, "would never have occurred to us, we of the generation of the War of Independence"). Levin shattered the taboos of the patriarchal code: bereaved parents, hitherto held sacrosanct, now came under attack; their values were not necessarily shared by the young, and wars were not always justified, particularly since it was the sons who paid the price and were usually the victims.

Already, in the aftermath of The Six Day War, Levin was attempting to strip away the veneer of fine words from national norms that had been neither challenged nor updated during the twenty years of Israel's existence. He achieved as much through the juxtaposition of colloquial syntax and elevated vocabulary (on the verge of the classical form of lamentation). On the one hand there are grandiloquent words, reflecting the rhetoric of public ceremonies, e.g., "graveside," "solitary," "flesh against flesh." At the same time such words appear within colloquial syntactical constructions, e.g., כשתעמוד ("when you stand over"), מאוד ערירי "very solitary"), which places the adverb before the adjective, reflecting a recent development in spoken Hebrew וזהו הזמן לבכות ("now is the time to cry"), מי שהקריב הייתי אני ("the one who made a sacrifice is me"). The presence of elevated diction within colloquial syntax casts an ironic light on the son's censure of the establishment. Levin also strikes back: his Abraham is not the hero portrayed in either the traditional exegesis of the *Aqedah* or in the rereading of previous literary generations. In the 1970s, for the first time, Abraham is mocked for being concerned solely with his own personal welfare. Before Levin and Amichai, and despite an earlier ironic approach towards the biblical Abraham, poets had not trivialized him in this manner.

Writers have generally found it easier to cloak Isaac, rather than Abraham, in the latest ideological fashion, since he is the paler figure in the biblical text. Levin's dispute is with neither the biblical text nor the intertextual tradition, but is directed against the contemporary use of the myth by the establishment and the collective consciousness. Levin cuts himself off from the mythical, historical, and collective dimensions of the *Aqedah* and looks instead for personal salvation. Abraham and Isaac are simply human beings. Neither is a symbol, nor part of historical destiny.

This change in ideological stance emerged after the Six Day War, but only in the texts of writers who were considered marginal and represented the anti-norm. One has to remember that after the Six Day War, the most voluble voices heard, especially in שִׂיחַ לוֹחֲמִים (*The Seventh Day*),[41] which became the canonic text of the period, were voices that sanctified sacrifice, particularly since the perspective was now one of destruction. The theme of bereavement was also treated with reverence and respect. Voices like Levin's, which were deemed subversive after the 1967 Six Day war, became more normative in the wake of the 1973 Yom Kippur war, and more volumble in the protest poetry penned during the 1982 war in Lebanon. Thus the study of the *Aqedah* as a test case can reflect a literary evolution from anti-norm to norm, from the margins to the center. Levin's work was considered anti-norm after the Six Day War, while after the Yom Kippur War and the war in Lebanon, it became such an integral part of the canon that it was included for study in the Israeli school curriculum. Poetry acts as a seismograph of social change, detecting hidden currents even before they surface. Poetry outscoops the newspapers. If you want to discover what a nation thinks, go to its literature.

After the Yom Kippur War, the *Aqedah* syndrome acquired an overwhelming significance in the consciousness of the Israeli people. Perhaps for the first time, there was a feeling that the very existence of the state was in jeopardy. The exceedingly large number of casualties and the possibility that even the state might become a victim combined in the consciousness of the people to give the *Aqedah* a symbolism suggesting global cosmic catastrophe. An intense expression of this feeling reverberates in a volume of poems by Avot Yeshurun, *The Syrian-African Rift*. The following 'הַשִּׁיר עַל הָאַפְרִיקִים' ("The Poem on the Africs") relates to the war with Egypt.

פְּלוּצִים נִפְתְּחָה דֶּלֶת. חַיָּל מָשַׁךְ אִישׁ מִלוּאִים הַחוּצָה.
פָּשַׁט אֶת הַטַּלִּית מֵרְחוֹב לִרְחוֹב וּמַקְשִׁיב לְסִפּוּר הַחַיָּל.
הָלַךְ עִם הַחַיָּל חָתוּל וְחָתוּל
וְלֶחִי וְלֶחִי.

הָלְכוּ שְׁנֵי הַמִּלוּאִאִימְנִיקִים אֶל הַשֶּׁבֶר
הַסּוּרִי אַפְרִיקָנִי: בָּאתְ אֵלֵינוּ לִבְרֹחַ מִן הַלָּבָן.
אֲבָל שָׁאַתָּה תִּהְיֶה הַנָּבָל? מָאוּס לִי הַמָּוֶת
כִּי אַפְרִיקִי בְּיָדֶיךָ.

יֵשׁ לָנוּ בְּעָיָה שֶׁל עֲקֵדַת יִצְחָק.
וְלָכֶם, כְּסָבוּר, עֲקֵדַת יִצְחָק.
לָנוּ זֶה יוֹצֵא כְּרַחֵם אָב עַל בָּנִים.
לָכֶם זֶה יוֹצֵא כְּרַחֵם אָב עַל עַצְמוֹ.

Plump a door opens. A soldier pulled a reservist outside.
Straightened the *tallith* from street to street and listening to the soldier's story.
Walked with the soldier cat and cat
and cheek and cheek.

The two reservist guys went to the Syrian-
African Rift: You came to escape the white.
But you be the villain? Loathsome to me is death
because an Afric's in your grip.

We have a problem of a sacrifice of Isaac.
And yours, you're inclined to think, the sacrifice of Isaac.
For us it comes out as a father has mercy on children.
For you it comes out as a father has mercy on himself.[42]

Even the title of the book testifies to a foreboding of catastrophe and disaster, as though a primal geological rift has appeared, since the poet exploits the ambiguity of the word שֶׁבֶר to signify both "rift" and "disaster." The Syrian African Rift runs from Lake Victoria through East Africa by way of the Red Sea and along the Jordan Valley, until it reaches Syria; and the

Yom Kippur War was mainly fought between Israel and two Arab states: Syria, and Egypt, which lies in Africa. Indeed, the war is now considered to have been a Syrian African disaster.

The Syrian African Rift is explicitly mentioned while using the enjambment between the word שֶׁבֶר ("rift") and *Syrian African* on the other, in order to emphasize the catastrophe. The opening line introduces the foreboding catastrophe through the use of a "Yeshurunite" original word, פְּלוֹצִים, which resonates with the Hebrew word פַּלָּצוּת ("horror," "monstrosity"), combined with the German *plötzlich*, meaning "suddenly." The sense of catastrophe is magnified by Yeshurun's special and ungrammatical syntax, full of pits and pitfalls, fusing different linguistic registers—usually Yiddish, Arabic, Polish, and here Yiddish at the outset. The lack of grammatical meaning and the syntactic collisions enable him to create free rhythms as in jazz and make surprising combinations such as "walked with the soldier cat and cat cheek and cheek."

The poem opens with a call to fight at the front. The protagonists are a soldier and a veteran whom he summons. This reading is implied in several ways: in the Yiddish of the one who opens the door, removing the prayer shawl that he wears at home, and the brutal manner in which the soldier drags him outside. The tension between the two is conveyed by the way they walk "cat and cat," like two suspicious rivals. Tension mounts, and is further intensified by the exchange of words between them, heard as a dialogue, in which the soldier aims to cast blame on the old veteran and finishes by referring to the Binding of Isaac. One possible interpretation is "You who came from Europe, from its snow or its death, how did you become the villain?" The linguistic play in Hebrew between לָבָן ("white") and נָבָל ("villain") conjures up the accusation that the old man, who signifies the father, is responsible for the soldier's loathsome death. And this is "because an Afrik's in your grip," which may be an allusion to the Israeli conquest of Sinai. Another intertext that may surface through the word "white" is the description of God as פַּחַד יִצְחָק in the biblical episode relating Jacob's flight from his father-in-law, Laban the Aramean. That flight may also evoke the father's escape from Europe.

The final stanza comprises the old man's words of self-defense as he presents both the position of the fathers—לָנוּ ("for us") and the stance of the sons—לָכֶם ("for you"). The father sees "a problem of a sacrifice of Isaac" in a nonspecific generalized way. From the father's point of view, the *Aqedah* is the story of a father's pity for his son; he is compelled to act because of God's command. However, as far as the son is concerned, the father pitied only himself, because he feared God (in the original narrative) or he feared losing the state with which he identified himself. Thus a cruel watershed is reached in the interpretation of the *Aqedah*: the son, who is bound, blames the father for the latter's egoistic motives.

Thus what was considered anti-norm in Levin's work after the Six Day War is not only normative after the Yom Kippur War but appears in the work of the veteran poet and grandfather of modern Israeli poetry, Avot Yeshurun—a poet who finds himself at the center of the contemporary canon.

The enduring power of myth is evinced even in its rejection. The War in Lebanon shattered many national myths. Voices of dissent became audible as poets protested against current events by questioning the moral message of the biblical *Aqedah*. This, however, is a large theme that deserves to be examined in its own right.

As in the biblical drama, fate arrives and once again sets on the stage the specter of a violent confrontation between the Hebrew settler and the land's native inhabitants. This time, however, the natives are not the Canaanites but the sons of Ishmael, and this adds fuel to the myth of the *Aqedah*. The collision between prophetic justice and the conscience of Diaspora Jewry finds poignant expression in the poetry of Avot Yeshurun. "The Holocaust of European Jewry and the Holocaust of the Arabs in the Land of Israel is the same Holocaust of the Jewish people: together they stare us in the face."[43] From here, the way is short to the exchange of Ishmael for the bound Isaac. Indeed, in his long poem 'הוּנָא מַחַטַטְתִּי', an Arabic radio identification call, a transformation of this kind takes place:

הֲיַעֲלוּ לַעֲקֵדָה צְחַא־צִיחַ?
יְ שְׁ מָ עֵ א ל הוּא הַבֵּן שֶׁהוּחַס.
הוּא הַבֵּן - הוּא מַלְאָךְ הַמַּבְטִיחַ.
וּמַלְאָךְ־לְהַבְטִיחַ לֹא חָס.

Will the parched one be sacrificed?
I s h m a e l is the son who was spared,
He is the son—he is the promising angel,
And the angel—to promise spares not.[44]

In other words, the angel who promised that Ishmael would be the father of a nation did not spare him when he was bound on the altar. In the memory of the Hebrew reader, these lines evoke a dialogue with the earlier verse of Lamdan's 'בַּחַמְסִין' ("Hot Spell"). (*Hamsin* is literally "fifty" in Arabic, from the notion that there are fifty scorching days every year.) In the following lines from Lamdan's epic poem 'מַסָדָה', we read:

אֵי שָׂרָה כִּי תֵּבְךְ לִבְנָהּ יִצְחָק
אֲשֶׁר כָּל יְהָבוֹ הָשְׁלַךְ פֹּה
עַל מוֹרָאוֹ שֶׁל הַיְשִׁימוֹן?

וְתַחַת שִׂיחַ־יָתוֹם בְּמִדְבַּר־מִקְלָט
לֹא בֶן הַמִּצְרִית הָשְׁלַךְ -
פֹּה בַּצָּמָא יִתְעַלֵּף יִצְחָק,
זֶרַע אַבְרָהָם וְשָׂרָה!

Where is Sarah, who weeps for her son Isaac,
Whose fate was entrusted here
To the dreaded wasteland?

And beneath a solitary bush in the desert-refuge
It was not the Egyptian woman's son—who was cast here
It is Isaac who will faint with thirst,
The seed of Abraham and Sarah![45]

Once again we encounter Isaac and Ishmael in the land of the patriarchs. But whereas Lamdan sends Isaac out to search for water and shade and leads him to the tortured desert of Ishmael, "the son of the Egyptian woman," Yeshurun leads Ishmael to the *Aqedah* and spares him. Here are the two basic moral and ideological perspectives of Zionism that have shaped its narratives. Like the other moral and ideological tensions mentioned above, they are sustained by a reservoir of metaphors from the *Aqedah*.

The continuous use of the biblical *Aqedah* suggests two different directions in which modern Hebrew literature is developing. One follows the current of protest against the political establishment, and the other, no less significant—deeply affected by the Six Day War and the Yom Kippur War, both of which starkly confronted Israeli society with the danger of total annihilation—is a fatalistic identification of the Israeli experience with the Holocaust. Modern Israeli writers have progressively rediscovered the ambivalence of Jewish existence and the enormous complexity of Jewish identity. The condition of the Jews may have changed, but not the Jewish condition.

In his epic 1956 saga, ימי צקלג ("The Days of Ziklag"), S. Yizhar—perhaps the most important writer of his generation—places the following words in the mouth of a battling soldier during the War of Independence and foreshadows the moral dilemmas expressed by future generations of Hebrew poets:

Who created such a bloody world? And you can't live without giving life or taking life.... I hate Abraham who goes to sacrifice Isaac. What right has he over Isaac, let him sacrifice himself. I hate the God who sent him to sacrifice and besieged him.... I hate that Isaac is nothing but an experiment between Abraham and his God. The self-sanctification of the God through the sacrifice of Isaac–I hate that too...bastards–what do the sons need to die for?[46]

*　*　*

In the original story the sacrifice is averted. For historians and theologians, the Binding of Isaac is the Jewish paradigm of redemption and salvation, forever pitted against the Christian paradigm of sacrifice. Mordechai Rotenberg distinguishes between these two paradigms:

> 1. The dialectic paradigm in which the idealisation of the filicidal killing–sacrificing of the son–Jesus, may trigger progress via the Oedipal elimination of the father's generation, so that the son comes to rule instead of the father.
> 2. The dialogic paradigm that idealizes Isaac's "patricidal" faith in a last-minute avoidance of Abraham's "filicidal" pressure to facilitate continuity of the son ruling after the father.[47]

Rotenberg concludes that "unlike Freud's Oedipal castrating, sword-threatening continuity, which triggers patricide, Abraham's *Aqedah*-sword must be understood as an urging-immunizing sword of Damocles assuring dialogic faith in the promised continuity that enhances investments in progress in spite of, and even when "a sharp sword is laid upon the neck.""[48]

But in modern Hebrew literature–as indeed, in some midrashic traditions–the *Aqedah* has remained a paradigm of sacrifice only, deriving its centrality and psychological force from the rooted perception of an ever real and ongoing sacrifice of the Jewish people in history. While the biblical tale refuses "to opt for finality or closure on the level of consciousness,"[49] and remains a permanently open story, modern Hebrew poetry has turned the story into a closed paradigm in which Abraham can never come down from the mountain and return home. The transformations that occur in the minds of the participants are irreversible. However, while the modern Israeli paradigm is closed, the capacity of the language in which it is couched to generate new and surprising meanings reopens it.

This generative quality of the story serves to create the master metaphor for the Zionist narrative. The abstract model is not deconstructed, only the ideological and psychological patterns drawn from it. Gradually the model loses its meaning. Causality disappears, and with it the telos of the model.

What is left is a sense of guilt and of walking on the brink of an abyss; a notion of experience as trial and a failure to endure that trial, a failure that in turn provokes a sense of guilt and of mortal danger. In the modern text, trial as guilt replaces Kierkegaard's *Fear and Trembling.* For a moment it seems that the Israeli poets are about to step out of history and that their meta-poetic stage signals a post traumatic stage. Yet in the decades since the Six Day War, the poets themselves are born with "a knife in their hearts" and even the wish to step out of Zionist history seems doomed to revert to the old Jewish paradigms. Studying rewritings of the *Aqedah* in the eighties and nineties might shed more light on such processes.

In many ways, the interpretation of the *Aqedah* in modern Hebrew poetry is akin to Ramban's typological reading of the Scriptures—that is, as prophecy decreed by events, a sort of miniature diagram delineating future circumstances. The deeds of the fathers determine the fate of their sons, מַעֲשֵׂה אָבוֹת סִימָן לְבָנִים.[50] Modern Israeli poetry, in all its diverse manifestations, perpetuates the deterministic character of the *Aqedah* as if through this trial, contemporary history were being shaped. Current political or even personal events are merely an enactment of the great archetype—the realization of a possibility latent in the biblical narrative. "They are born with a knife in their hearts." Thus we witness a closed circular story: endless repetition, rather than development. The question of the poetic and political incarnations the myth is likely to undergo in the coming years is one to trouble the mind.

A Modern Mystical Experience

Intertextuality and Deconstruction in
Israeli Women's Poetry

Introduction

In recent decades, with the burgeoning of women's writing in Israel, we witness resourceful women's texts, saturated with echoes from a rich literary tradition. It has been argued that the initial entry of women writers into the arena of Hebrew literature in the twenties was marked by limited use of cultural sources.[1] However, the wealth of cultural reference and allusions that women had renounced for sociological, ideological, and other reasons returns to enrich their writing in contemporary Hebrew poetry. This increasing reverberation is the result of the feminist revolution and serves as a weapon in it. A poignant example of this literary development is exemplified in the poetry of Yona Wallach.

One can scarcely discuss the role of women in Hebrew poetry without stressing the centrality of Wallach in its formation. Without reference to her, one can only speak in general terms of the dramatic development of the feminist revolution and view the leap made by women poets during the 1980s as a response to global, social, cultural and stylistic developments.

Wallach belongs to that rare breed of writers who set the agenda for future literary generations; she is one of those iconoclastic poets who challenge boundaries and examine new dimensions of language and love, of expression and feeling. She revolutionized Hebrew poetry by daring to present the figures in her poems as provocative and sexually open, or as women who do not accept the usual socio-cultural status of the female libido, or as wounded and rejected souls who retreat into mystery and madness. On first reading, her poems appear to be fragmentary, uncontrolled, wild, and incoherent, but on closer examination they reveal themselves as surprisingly intellectual and intricately structured.[2]

Wallach died in 1985 at the age of forty-one, but her poetry stamped itself indelibly on the consciousness of the Israeli public, even during her lifetime. Her poems were set to music composed by the best Israeli musicians and performed by the country's most popular singers. She often spoke at events where she was invited to give readings of her work, and her deep musical voice was frequently heard on radio programs. Wallach took on the persona both of prophet and the accursed, which is what a woman poet should be in the romantic tradition. In fact she became a cult figure.

One of her poems, called 'תְּפִלִּין' ("phylacteries"), reads: "...I shall put on tefillin / ...wrap them about my hands / Wrap them over the pleasurable places on my body...."[3] Its publication raised a stormy debate in the Israeli Parliament and brought her to the center of public controversy for daring to associate one of the most sacrosanct of male ritual practices with highly suggestive sexual imagery. Her turbulent lifestyle and eccentric personality attracted much attention. She frequently experimented with psychedelic drugs, which may have exacerbated her repeated bouts of mental break-down. Madness and disease became motifs in many of her poems. She is one of the few contemporary Hebrew poets about whom book-length biog-raphies have been written.[4] Recently a monograph dedicated to her poetry was published.[5] Some critics compare her poetry to that of Sylvia Plath. Others maintain that her voice was unique, but even those critics who are less than enthusiastic are struck by her innovative powers. Since the 1960s she has been a source of inspiration and still serves as a literary model for two generations of women poets.

Even readers drawn to the personal tone of Wallach's work find it at times puzzling and hermetic. Her innovative verse was initially seen as self-con-tained to the point of being almost solipsistic. Critics believed that her newly minted myths were unrelated to well known cultural sources—e.g. to He-brew canonical texts.

In this chapter, however, I wish to present a different view, based on theories of intertextuality and on readings, interpretations, and methodol-ogies taken from women's literary theory. My argument is that Wallach's work epitomizes a historical-cultural process and that her poetry does wrestle with ghosts from the past. Moreover, it is through intertextual dialogue with canonic texts—Hebrew and others—that she explores her identity most con-vincingly.

The abundance of intertextual references in Israeli women's writing in the past decades is the product of an historical development. As a result of this cultural and political process, Israeli women poets have begun to echo and incorporate canonical texts more extensively. Some critics argue that women's writing has always been laden with intertextuality.[6] It is my con-tention that the revolution in Israeli Women's modern writing is character-ized by the scope and functionality of these referential inclusions, which have proliferated and become much more organic. This functional and rich enactment of the cultural echo chamber is a distinct marker of these women's artistic achievement.

Post-Structuralist discourse teaches us that our lives are shaped by the texts we read and that our consciousness is determined by them. This per-spective is of special importance for any group interested in forming a new kind of self-awareness, especially for female artists who aim to deconstruct male discourse and its more chauvinistic narratives. A new women's liter-ature is, therefore, an attempt to challenge the hegemony of male thought, which has shaped reality for men and women alike. This endeavor is actualized by means of appropriating one of the male's most significant power centers: the story. The strength of the story is derived from its function as an organizer of human experience.

Alicia Ostricker states that women writers have had to become *voleuses de langue* ("thieves of language") in order to invade the "oppressor's language" and to rewrite their own myths to transform the "Law of the Father."[7] Thus the rewriting of mythology is seen as a means for the transformation of identity as well as culture.

This critical observation also accords with intertextual theories: in both theoretical approaches, the intertext—be it myth, legend or any other topos— will be transformed into a newly created text, with the distinction that a feminist rewriting of myth will generally be political in nature. Poet-critic Adrienne Rich has argued that when women write strongly as women they do so to subvert and transform their lives and the literature they inherit.[8]

Intertextual methodology can cast light on the strategies by which the act of "stealing the language" and rewriting the myths is performed. Michael Riffaterre argues that the ultimate meaning of a text and its literariness depend on the reader's ability to identify and activate "the web of functions that constitutes and regulates the relationships between text and intertext."[9] The intertext is a multiplicity of other texts, interwoven into the current one through a mesh of "connectives" (a neologism coined by Riffaterre). According to Riffaterre, the connectives act as signposts that guide the reader in the direction of the intertexts. The awareness that intertexts exist will be prompted in the reader by these indicators and ought to trigger a response in him or her. Readers should then be able to identify the intertext in question, or simply sense its absence.

In this way a tension is created between the reader and the text, and a need is felt by the reader to locate the intertext and decipher the relationships between it and the text. The reader becomes an active participant in the creation and production of new meanings. The outcome of such an encounter can be so important that the meaning of both text and intertext are consequently transformed. Such new interpretations are always defined and constrained by the intertext. When this is not immediately identified or remains undiscovered, readers can only enjoy a limited response to the text itself.

One of the strategies employed by feminist writers is to revise "gendered imagery." Hebrew can be deconstructed easily since its grammatical structure is gender-oriented and gender-determined. All its nouns, pronouns, adjectives, and verbs are either masculine or feminine, sometimes both.

Wallach states in one of her poems that Hebrew is a "sex maniac" language.[10]

Wallach "steals the language" by rewriting biblical myths as well as other Western cultural archetypes. Her revisionist mythmaking serves as a vehicle for defining and exploring femininity and identity. By playing such myths and archetypes against one another, her poems become literary loci for original and daring dialogues.

However, since her poems deconstruct the intertexts so radically that they become barely discernible, these dialogues are often elusive. Moreover, the extreme liberties she takes with gender and syntax also affect the legibility of the text, making her intertext doubly difficult to spot—a provocative and frustrating state of affairs for the reader. Yet it is mainly through the intertextual process that she demarcates and proclaims her own creative space. Thus, for a reader who is not too easily given to despair, the uneasy relationship between poem and intertext can serve as an incentive to search for the latter, in order to impose some cognitive order on the former and so create richer and more complex levels of meaning.

The Ecstasy of Saint Teresa

We now turn to Wallach's poem 'צָרוֹתֶיהָ שֶׁל דּוֹנָה תֶּרֶזָה' ("The Troubles of Donna Teresa"), which can be seen as a test case for demonstrating how intertextual strategies evoke an idea of female identity in contemporary Israeli women's writing:

צָרוֹתֶיהָ הַיְפֵהפִיּוֹת שֶׁל דּוֹנָה תֶּרֶזָה
לֹא שׁוֹבְבוּ אֶת לִבִּי הַיּוֹם
נִלְאֵיתִי בְּעֵינַי מְאֹד
נָקַלּוֹתִי שָׁנִים
שֶׁבָּהֶן בְּלִי הֶרֶף
נְחִירַיִךְ רוֹטְטִים דּוֹנָה תֶּרֶזָה
הֲלֹא תֹאמְרִי דַּי בְּרִגְשַׁיִךְ
בֵּיתָהּ יְסָדַתְהוּ בִּבְדֹלַח
וְרִכְּכַתְהוּ בִּקְטִיפָה
רְבוּצָה בְּיָפְיִ
וְעוֹד נְחִירֶיהָ רוֹטְטִים
קַלְגַּסִּים מַעֲלֶיהָ בִּעֵף
נוֹקְשׁוֹת פְּנִימוֹת נַעֲלוֹתֵיהֶם
וְדוֹנָה תֶּרֶזָה אוֹסֶפֶת דִּיּוֹת
מְאַגֶּדֶת רַגְלוֹתֵיהֶם לִמְשִׁיחָה
יְעָצַנִי לִבִּי לָקוּם עָלֶיהָ
וְסַכִּינָה בְּפוֹסְפוֹר מְשַׁחַתְהוּ

שֶׁאֲנִי קִלַּלְתָּךְ לְעוֹלָם וָעֶד
לָאֵטָה קְרוּעָה דּוֹנָה תֶּרֶזָה
שֶׁכַּלְתִי לְעוֹלָם יְדַעְתִּיהָ
תָּמִיד מַחֲזִיקָה זְכוּכִית מְפֻיַחַת
בְּמִקְרֶה שֶׁהַשֶׁמֶשׁ

Donna Teresa's gorgeous troubles
Did not captivate my heart today
I seem to have grown very weary
I despised myself all these years
While ceaselessly
Your nostrils quiver Donna Teresa
Have you not had enough of your sensations
Her house she set in crystal
And softened it with velvet
Wallowing in beauty
And still her nostrils quiver
Legionaries above her in swift flight
The insteps of their boots beating
And Donna Teresa collects falcons
Binding their feet for anointment
My heart advised me to rise up against her
She anointed her dagger with phosphorus
That I be your curse for ever and ever
Whispered ruptured Donna Teresa
That my eternal bride I know
Always holding up a smoked glass
Just in case the sun[11]

This poem appeared in Wallach's first volume of verse, published in 1966, entitled דְּבָרִים (meaning both "words" and "things").[12] To Israeli readers, many of the women portrayed in the poems have exotic names–for example, Cornelia, Christina, and Antonia. Almost all of these women are powerless victims, particularly in confrontation with male characters. Thus they generally choose to shrink into their own internal realities, avoiding action and leaving no real mark on the world around them. In contrast with such characters, Donna Teresa stands out most forcibly, since she is the most active character in the entire collection. She builds an exquisite house, where she luxuriates. Its interior is decorated sumptuously with "crystal" and "velvet," while her "nostrils quiver" with delight. She collects falcons– appropriating a chivalric male pursuit–and, when threatened, "curses" and is prepared to fight back against her oppressor. Despite her activity, she loses neither individuality nor identity, unlike various other female characters in Wallach's poetry. The most telling definition of Donna Teresa (as the embodiment of full and authentic female experience) appears in the expression רְבוּצָה בְּיָפְיִ ("wallowing in beauty") (רְבוּצָה also means "crouching in an animal-like way").

In my reading of the poem, I find two distinct voices: that of a female juxtaposed with the predominant speech of a male. The poem begins with an interior monologue, as the male cries out: "Your gorgeous troubles /Did not enchant my heart today…." Androgynous vocalization, the melding of male and female identities so distinctive in Wallach's poetry, surfaces in this double voice of the narrator. This strategy—questioning the boundaries of gender—creates constant shifts of perspective that blur the clarity of the poem.

Donna Teresa's impulsive, ecstatic character ("with her ever quivering nostrils"), seems to enrage the male speaker most, as he protests: "Have you not had enough of your sensations." Donna Teresa's intensity acts upon the speaker, shattering his fragile self-image, ("I seem to have grown very weary / I…despised myself all these years…"). Having harbored such thoughts for so long, he is now prepared to take violent action: "My heart advised me to rise up against her."

Even at this stage, Donna Teresa does not succumb, but fights back: "She anointed her dagger with phosphorus." The outcome, although not specified, seems to be tragic as the utter incompatibility of these two characters leads them, with apparent inevitability, to a terrible end. The ambiguous final lines of the poem imply that Donna Teresa triumphs in her struggle against him, as she is left holding a "smoky glass" up to the sun, possibly in self-defense so as not to be blinded by her adversary, or perhaps for incendiary purposes, which shows her to be intrinsically a warrior.

The question of how such a unique character came into being, in marked contrast with the other female figures in the volume, may now be considered. The answer seems to stem from the extremely sophisticated dialogue the poem conducts with three canonic texts, in each of which an individualized, dominant woman is central. The three texts are: (a) Saint Teresa's mystical vision; (b) the biblical acrostic poem known as אֵשֶׁת־חַיִל or "Praises of the Virtuous Woman" (Proverbs 31:10-31); and (c) the Greek myth of Amor and Psyche.

Teresa de Jesus, Santa Teresa, also known as Teresa of Avila, captured the imagination of Yona Wallach and evoked within her a deep sense of empathy with this extraordinary woman. Saint Teresa's mystical leanings and immense charisma made her one of the most popular saints, not only in her own time but also in ours. She lived in Spain in the second half of the sixteenth century, and at the age of twenty-nine experienced an intense mystical revelation, as a result of which she resolved to introduce contemplative practices, emphasizing the inner life, into the Carmelite orders she founded. Such radical changes met with many obstacles, due to the antagonism of the entrenched male establishment.

Nevertheless, Saint Teresa succeeded in realizing her ideals. She gave expression to her religious and mystical experiences in a number of essays and books that were to become part of the canonic Catholic mystical tradition. One of her major works, which recounts the foundation of the convents of St. Joseph at Avila in 1562, is entitled *Book of Foundations of Saint Teresa of Jesus.*[13] A glance at her texts shows Teresa's style to be fervent, impassioned, almost delirious. Her language is described by scholars as "simple, archaic and extremely figurative, often lacking in precision and clarity, but always attractive and fascinating. She expanded the meaning of words until they became allusive expressions of visions and experiences that transcend language."[14] With the exception of the term "simple," such a description may apply equally well to Wallach's poetic diction. Since an intimate communication with God is such a profound constituent of her poetry, it is no wonder that the figure of the Christian mystic and her writings held such an appeal for Wallach.[15]

In one of Saint Theresa's most famous visions, in *Life and Other Books*, the Saint describes the appearance of God's angel:

> In his hand I saw a golden spear and at its iron tip there appeared to be a point of fire. This he plunged into my heart several times so that it penetrated my entrails. [.....] The sweetness caused by this intense pain is so extreme that one cannot possibly wish it to cease....This is not a physical, but a spiritual pain, though the body has some share in it—even a considerable pain."[16]

This vision was faithfully sculpted by the Italian artist Giovanni Lorenzo Bernini (1598-1680) in every detail and is perhaps the most celebrated of his works.[17] The sculpture stands in the Cornaro Chapel in the Church of Santa Maria della Vittoria in Rome, and it is highly likely that it (together with Teresa's original writings) was the immediate source of inspiration for Wallach's poem. The first process of signification is thus produced through an intricate dialogue developing between the two works of art, the sculpture being the first "intertext."

Umberto Eco claims that transposing from one artistic medium to an-

other amounts to reviving "a dead metaphor": "In shifting from one semiotic system to another, a dead metaphor becomes an inventing one anew."[18] In many ways, Wallach's poem is a realization of just such "a dead metaphor." Santa Teresa's ecstatic state, conveyed in the written evocation of the vision, as well as elements of Bernini's sculpture, are together captured in the poem. To an observer of the sculpture, the stone nostrils do indeed appear to quiver, and Bernini's Santa Teresa is best described as overwhelmed by "gorgeous troubles." Her ecstatic facial expression, the position of the angel, and the fact that he delicately lifts the gown near her breast, leave no doubt as to the erotic overtones in this sculpture. The reader of the vision, like the observer of the sculpture, would find it difficult not to believe that Teresa's ecstasy was erotic as well as religious. Indeed, Bernini is renowned for his secular/religious representations. While the Saint's "gorgeous troubles" derive from her seduction by the angel, the speaker of the poem remains unmoved, as he emphatically declares: "Donna Teresa's gorgeous troubles failed to enchant my heart today."

It is as if the poem continues in time beyond the moment in which the sculpture has frozen into shape. The sculpture emphasizes the spatial opposition between Teresa and the angel: while she is lying down, he stands above her; while his arms are slightly raised to lift the folds of her dress, she swoons; his face expresses joy and complete consciousness of what is taking place, while she appears passive and withdrawn. This contrast creates no tension in the sculpture. On the contrary, that tension effects the ecstatic experience. When transferred in all its intensity to Wallach's poem, the polarity creates a dramatic role reversal between its male and female figures. It is Donna Teresa who becomes the aggressor, physically assuming the male role. Symbolically, sexual control is transferred to her, since she is the one clutching the dagger.

In Wallach's text the original vision is fundamentally dismantled though all its central elements are present in the poem. The order and logic of the intertext are deconstructed, leaving the absent elements to form a completely new puzzle. The ecstatic sensuality of the female figure is present, but unlike what appears in the sculpture, it does not stem from the strength of the male. Rather, it is an innate characteristic of the woman, whom the male speaker is unable to confront. God's angel has not completely disappeared, but has instead been transformed into the demonic figure who hovers above Donna Teresa as she holds the angel's dagger of love. The pain, which was both spiritual and replete with orgasmic pleasure, by the close of the poem has become physical, tangible, violent, and destructive, as ruptured Donna Teresa whispers: "That I be your curse forever."

The relationship of Wallach's poem to the sculpture is, therefore, dialectical. It is clear that there is an absorption of deep structures that exists both in the vision and in the sculpture (such as the ecstasy and sensuality of the female figure). Moreover, the depiction of Donna Teresa's unique persona in the poem is possible only because Santa Teresa's physical presence is embodied in the sculpture. Thus, Wallach's poem becomes a sort of ekphrasis–defined by W.J.T. Mitchell as "a verbal representation of a visual representation."[19] "Ekphrastic poetry," claims Mitchell, "is a genre in which texts encounter their own semiotic 'others,' those rivals, alien modes of representation called visual, graphic, plastic, or 'spatial arts.'"[20] In identifying the sculpture as an intertext, a new object, which is an image-text, is created. Consequently, a relationship of struggle and contest is generated between the two texts. Gender also energizes the dialectic of the image-text: the tension can also be seen in a socio-political context, since the sculpture presents the male perspective, whereas the poem reflects the view of the female. Thus the relationship between image and text can be read as one of struggle and confrontation with hegemony.

Furthermore, the dialectic between the poem and the sculpture, which establishes the modern text as ekphrastic poetry, exemplifies poststructuralist thought, according to which the relationship between verbal and visual media is not one of similarity and opposition, but of struggle and confrontation. In other words, relationships can be based upon a wide variety of non-binary oppositions, such as tension and dissonance.[21]

The Virtuous Woman

Similar processes of signification are at work in the dialogue with another canonic text, namely the acrostic section of Proverbs (31:10), known in Hebrew as 'אֵשֶׁת־חַיִל ("A Woman of Valor"). Here the processes of signification are more complex and subversive, although on a first reading it is hard to identify any obvious links between the ancient and modern texts. However, a close reading reveals an extensive web of fine and delicate threads that bind them.

אֵשֶׁת־חַיִל מִי יִמְצָא
וְרָחֹק מִפְּנִינִים מִכְרָהּ.
בָּטַח בָּהּ לֵב בַּעְלָהּ
וְשָׁלָל לֹא יֶחְסָר.
גְּמָלַתְהוּ טוֹב וְלֹא־רָע
כֹּל יְמֵי חַיֶּיהָ.
דָּרְשָׁה צֶמֶר וּפִשְׁתִּים
וַתַּעַשׂ בְּחֵפֶץ כַּפֶּיהָ.

הָיְתָה כָּאֳנִיּוֹת סוֹחֵר
מִמֶּרְחָק תָּבִיא לַחְמָהּ.
וַתָּקָם בְּעוֹד לַיְלָה
וַתִּתֵּן טֶרֶף לְבֵיתָהּ
וְחֹק לְנַעֲרֹתֶיהָ.
זָמְמָה שָׂדֶה וַתִּקָּחֵהוּ
מִפְּרִי כַפֶּיהָ נָטְעָה כָּרֶם.
חָגְרָה בְעוֹז מָתְנֶיהָ
וַתְּאַמֵּץ זְרוֹעֹתֶיהָ.
טָעֲמָה כִּי־טוֹב סַחְרָהּ
לֹא־יִכְבֶּה בַלַּיְלָה נֵרָהּ.
יָדֶיהָ שִׁלְּחָה בַכִּישׁוֹר
וְכַפֶּיהָ תָּמְכוּ פָלֶךְ.
כַּפָּהּ פָּרְשָׂה לֶעָנִי
וְיָדֶיהָ שִׁלְּחָה לָאֶבְיוֹן.
לֹא־תִירָא לְבֵיתָהּ מִשָּׁלֶג
כִּי כָל־בֵּיתָהּ לָבֻשׁ שָׁנִים.
מַרְבַדִּים עָשְׂתָה־לָּהּ
שֵׁשׁ וְאַרְגָּמָן לְבוּשָׁהּ.
נוֹדָע בַּשְּׁעָרִים בַּעְלָהּ
בְּשִׁבְתּוֹ עִם־זִקְנֵי־אָרֶץ.
סָדִין עָשְׂתָה וַתִּמְכֹּר
וַחֲגוֹר נָתְנָה לַכְּנַעֲנִי.
עוֹז־וְהָדָר לְבוּשָׁהּ
וַתִּשְׂחַק לְיוֹם אַחֲרוֹן.
פִּיהָ פָּתְחָה בְחָכְמָה
וְתוֹרַת־חֶסֶד עַל־לְשׁוֹנָהּ.
צוֹפִיָּה הֲלִיכוֹת בֵּיתָהּ
וְלֶחֶם עַצְלוּת לֹא תֹאכֵל.
קָמוּ בָנֶיהָ וַיְאַשְּׁרוּהָ
בַּעְלָהּ וַיְהַלְלָהּ.
רַבּוֹת בָּנוֹת עָשׂוּ חָיִל
וְאַתְּ עָלִית עַל־כֻּלָּנָה.
שֶׁקֶר הַחֵן וְהֶבֶל־הַיֹּפִי
אִשָּׁה יִרְאַת־יְהֹוָה הִיא תִתְהַלָּל.
תְּנוּ־לָהּ מִפְּרִי יָדֶיהָ
וִיהַלְלוּהָ בַשְּׁעָרִים מַעֲשֶׂיהָ.

Who can find a virtuous woman?
for her price is far above rubies.
The heart of her husband doth safely trust in her,

so that he shall have no need of spoil.
She will do him good and not evil
all the days of her life.
She seeketh wool, and flax,
and worketh willingly with her hands.
She is like the merchants' ships;
She bringeth her food from afar.
She riseth also while it is yet night,
and giveth meat to her household,
and a portion to her maidens.
She considereth a field and buyeth it:
with the fruit of her hands she planteth a vineyard.
She girdeth her loins with strength,
and strengtheneth her arms.
She perceiveth that her merchandise is good:
her candle goeth not out by night.
She layeth her hands to the spindle,
and her hands hold the distaff.
She stretcheth out her hand to the poor;
yea, she reacheth forth her hands to the needy.
She is not afraid of the snow for her household:
for all her household are clothed with scarlet.
She maketh her coverings of tapestry;
her clothing is silk and purple.
Her husband is known at the gates,
when he sitteth among the elders of the land.
She maketh fine linen and selleth it;
and delivereth girdles unto the merchants.
Strength and honor are her clothing;
and she shall rejoice in time to come.
She openeth her mouth with wisdom;
and in her tongue is the law of kindness.
She looketh well to the ways of her household,
and eateth not the bread of idleness.
Her children rise up, and call her blessed;
her husband also, and he praiseth her.
Many daughters have done virtuously,
but thou excellest them all.
Favour is deceitful, and beauty is vain:
but a woman that feareth the Lord shall be praised.

Give her of the fruit of her hands;
and let her own works praise her in the gates.

In the traditional Jewish home, these verses are recited on returning from the synagogue on Friday night by the head of the family to his wife, before the ritual meal is served. Indeed, 'אֵשֶׁת־חַיִל' is an integral part of the canonical, patriarchal tradition.

A mutual system of markers links the modern poem with the biblical 'אֵשֶׁת־חַיִל'. First, the virtuous woman is well-dressed—her clothing and that of her household is made of "silk and purple." Although she takes care of her home and person, physical beauty as such is eschewed as a feature of intrinsic worth. In Proverbs the poem ends as the male speaker declares שֶׁקֶר הַחֵן וְהֶבֶל־הַיֹּפִי ("Favor is deceitful, and beauty is vain").

The signifier "heart" has different functions within the two texts. In Wallach's poem the word carries subversive connotations: "Your gorgeous troubles did not capture my heart today," and "My heart advised me to rise up against her." However, "heart" in Proverbs is associated with praiseworthy qualities: "The heart of her husband doth safely trust in her."

Similarly, the term "rise" is used in contrasting ways. In Proverbs, it is associated with the commendable qualities of the virtuous woman, for she "riseth also while it is yet night" to attend to her responsibilities. It is also a token of respect: "Her children rise up, and call her blessed." But in Wallach's poem "rise" has violent and rebellious connotations and undertones: ("My heart advised me to rise up against her"). The man is enraged by the presence of a woman of Donna Teresa's stature.

One can also point to a euphonic parallelism between the poetic dictions of the ancient and modern texts, creating different forms of paronomasia; for example, מִפְּנִינִים / פְּנִימוֹת ("insteps/pearls")[22]; שָׁנִים / שָׁנִי ("silk/scarlet"); מִכְרָה / נְחִירֶיהָ ("nostrils/sells"), and several others. It should be noted that when Wallach characterizes Donna Teresa's actions, or actions taken against her, all the nouns assume the feminine gender, e.g., פְּנִימוֹת ("insteps"), a neologism coined by Wallach. She even chooses the rare biblical word for falcons דַּיּוֹת, a noun in the feminine and נְעָלוֹת ("boots") (Joshua 9:5), derived from נַעֲלָיִם in the masculine gender. Thus she composes her feminine narrative by exploiting its grammatical gender.

Both texts portray women of high standing. In Proverbs the wife is "a virtuous woman," whose "husband is known at the gates...when he sitteth among the elders of the land," while in Wallach's poem Teresa is entitled "Donna," a term of social esteem. Indeed, both texts establish very different icons of the female and femininity, as the text/intertext relationship stresses differences through similarity. In Proverbs the ideal Jewish wife is compliant, doing everything to advance the interests of her husband: she gets up early and works herself to the bone, then sells the merchandise she has made with her own hands so that he can sit leisurely at the city gates and chat with the elders of the town. No tension exists between the woman and her partner as she willingly subordinates herself to his interests. By contrast, the modern poem creates a new female identity through debate and argument with the biblical source, which it simultaneously absorbs and negates. The pervading atmosphere of *Donna Teresa* is tense, violent and dissonant, as the heroine refuses to perform the role demanded by the man, even at great cost to herself.

Through his depictions of the woman, the biblical poet sets in motion semantic fields related to the animal kingdom, to violence, and to war, reflected in the words שָׁלָל ("spoil"), טֶרֶף ("prey / food"), זָמְמָה ("schemed" / "contrived"), and עוֹז ("prowess"). Violence is evoked by representing the wife as a huntress who rises while it is yet night to provide food or to hunt for prey. Hunting and war-like traits are implied by the subtle definition of "a woman of valor."

The Wallach poem enacts a realization of this metaphor. The biblical חַיִל, which denotes "ingenuity/valor," is transfigured into "she anointed her dagger with phosphorous" in the modern text. The modern text activates the latent metaphor of "huntress," implied in the prototype of an ideal woman in the guise of an אֵשֶׁת־חַיִל. What was repressed in the biblical text becomes the focus of the modern poem. The intertextual process is marked by an inversion of symbolic values: in the biblical text the virtuous woman is compelled to provide food because of her obsessive concern with the survival of the family and home, while the modern woman is a falconer hunting for pure pleasure.

Although sensual beauty characterizes the figure of Donna Teresa, the "virtuous woman" is wholly preoccupied with spinning, weaving, planting, making and selling merchandise, etc. The sensuality absent in the biblical intertext becomes the *dominanta* in Wallach's poem. The biblical representation of womanhood distinguishes very clearly between orderly and demonic characteristics, both of which are solely associated with the woman's activities and possessions (טֶרֶף לְבֵיתָהּ), rather than with the subject herself. The shift from object to subject in the modern poem evokes a wild persona, witnessed by the way her nostrils quiver, in animal-like fashion.

Beauty as an end in itself is an immanent component of the new female identity. The virtuous woman also values beautiful things: she is not satisfied with simple woolen clothing, but strives and sweats to ensure that all her household are clothed with scarlet (שֵׁשׁ וְאַרְגָּמָן לְבוּשָׁהּ). She herself wears "silk and purple," while her house is hung with "tapestries." However, such aesthetic standards serve a purely functional purpose: namely, to provide for the family's needs. Thus, the biblical poet categorically denounces beauty at the closure: "Favour is deceitful, and beauty is vain."

The central metonymies in the two texts relate to body language, as can be seen in the use of the terms "hand" and "nostrils," respectively, and illustrate the enormous differences between the two women depicted. In Proverbs the metonymy יָדֶיהָ ("her hands"), or the palm of the hand appears in the Hebrew text as כַּפֶּיהָ and כַּפָּהּ. On one occasion the virtuous woman "worketh willingly with her hands," on another she "strengtheneth her arms"; "she layeth her hands to the spindle," and "stretcheth out her hand to the poor." The hand, or the palm of the hand, designates outward action and enterprise. By contrast, Donna Teresa's quivering nostrils are signs of the heroine's individual, autonomous autoerotic inner world, associated with wild sensuality and infinite passion.

This distinction between instrumentality and aestheticism may be further illustrated by comparing the signifier "house" in both texts. In Proverbs the house is functional and real, not to mention its place as the raison de etre of the virtuous woman's life. In contrast, Donna Teresa's house, echoing the "Book of Foundations" by Saint Teresa (see below), seems an enchanted and surreal backdrop for this exotic character.

Processes of absorption and negation take place in the morphological and euphonic constituents present in both texts. The pronominal suffix תְהוּ־, used in Proverbs, describes different functions associated with the virtuous woman; for example גְּמָלַתְהוּ ("she does him good, i.e. provides for him"). Wallach, however, deconstructs this euphonic feature, since the conclusion is a blanket term to cover all practical activities associated with the "virtuous woman." By contrast, in the modern poem, this euphonic feature emphasizes the activities pursued by Donna Teresa purely for pleasure, joy and delight, e.g. יְסָדַתְהוּ ("she built") her house in crystal. And רִבְּכַתְהוּ ("she softened/lined it") with velvet. The euphony of the long a and u vowels impart an archaic tone to the modern text, evoking resonances that complement the aesthetic delights associated with Donna Teresa's palace.

The verse אֵשֶׁת־חַיִל מִי יִמְצָא וְרָחֹק מִפְּנִינִים מִכְרָהּ ("Who can find a virtuous woman? For her price is far above rubies")[23] undergoes a fascinating process of deconstruction. The semantic field at work in this metaphor is commercial, as befits the businesslike character of the woman in Proverbs. Among other considerations, the biblical woman is held to be far more valuable than rare rubies or pearls. The commercial associations of the biblical text are deconstructed and radically altered in the modern poem to create richly seductive lines, as the word פְּנִינִים ("rubies") is broken into two parts, the semantic and the euphonic. By linking the semantic component to another precious material, בְּדֹלַח ("crystal"), it is transfigured. In its modern coupling it no longer finds itself associated with material worth, but rather as a referent to Donna Teresa's love of beauty. Yet the term פְּנִינִים ("rubies") has not disappeared. Its sound surfaces in the magical, surreal line: קַלְגַּסִּים מֵעָלֶיהָ בְּיָעָף / נוֹקְשׁוֹת פְּנִימוֹת נַעֲלוֹתֵיהֶם ("Legionaries above her in swift flight / The insteps [פְּנִימוֹת] of their boots beating.") The modern woman poet employs an elaborate type of paronomasia, changing the original text while still preserving the memory of the sound, modifying the orthography to lend the biblical text a newly created meaning. The noun פְּנִימוֹת signals to the reader that Proverbs is one of the intertexts of Wallach's poem.

Amor and Psyche

There is yet another canvas that the poem seems to overlay, namely the fable of Amor and Psyche, which provides a further mythical reading. The feasibility of such a reading is implied, I suggest, by the association of "knife" with "phosphorus" (essentially an element that emits light on reacting with air) in the weapon with which Donna Teresa fights. Such a combination calls to mind Psyche's attempt on the life of Amor while holding a knife and a lamp. Although the links between the two texts are weaker in this case, nonetheless the reading of Wallach's poem benefits by identifying the mythical story as another intertext. My reading is based on a psychoanalytic interpretation suggested by Erich Neumann in his 1956 study *Amor and Psyche: On the Development of the Feminine Element*.[24]

Besides other shared motifs, such as light and knife, beauty and ecstasy, the myth of Amor and Psyche resonates through the uncompromising fight against patriarchal, chauvinist love in the poem. Psyche may struggle against Amor's love, but it saves her from Aphrodite's fury. However, it leaves her imprisoned in a "luxurious jail," where she is forced to lose her keen sense of awareness in exchange for sexual satisfaction. She is allowed neither to look at her beloved's face during love-making, nor to meet with her sisters. Amor's palace is the locus where Psyche's development takes place at this stage. The sisters whom she meets, despite the ban, represent a layer in Psyche's soul that rebels against this type of subjugation. From the very beginning, Donna Teresa is not prepared to submit to patriarchal subjugation. Her luxurious palace is her home alone. She does not need a man in there—her nostrils quiver in delight, with or without him. Seen in the context of the ancient myth, however, one can understand the male speaker's expectations in the palace of Donna Teresa. He hopes that, like Amor's palace, her enchanted house will serve to constrain Teresa, completely enslaving her by erasing her individual identity. Thus he is disappointed when, even after the palace is built, her nostrils continue to "quiver" joyously, like a free, untamed animal. Donna Teresa, like Psyche, rebels against this attempt at male domination. However, whereas Psyche experiences a gradual process of awakening and is finally able to relate to the man honestly and emotionally without losing her female identity, Donna Teresa prefers to remain in her narcissistic bubble, foregoing any process of maturation. She concentrates entirely on her sensuous pleasures, personal achievements, and self-fulfillment, all of which she is not prepared to abandon, even for a profound, emotional, and reciprocal relationship with a man.

Like Donna Theresa—and unlike Amor in the myth—the male character in Wallach's poem is incapable of spiritual development. The myth's happy ending, contrary to Neumann's claim, is neither forced nor artificial, but a consequence of both Psyche's spiritual development and Amor's ability to cut himself free from patriarchal modes of thought and behavior. In contrast, it is the psychological immutability of the two characters in the Wallach poem that leads them to a tragic finale.

In the Greek myth, light, concentrated in a candle, symbolizes awareness and rationality. In the poem it is transfigured into phosphorus, which, as noted earlier, glows in air and comes to represent Donna Teresa's fighting spirit. The candle in the ancient myth has an autonomous status, while the knife is a loaded symbol: it is held by Psyche on her way to Amor and is an instrument of destruction. In Wallach's poem, the dagger becomes a symbol of self- defense ("She anointed her dagger with phosphorus"). Such a combination negates any cognitive differentiation and perhaps expresses, more than anything else, the difference between the two women, Psyche and Donna Teresa.

The intertextual space created by the myth of Psyche and Amor may help us to interpret the last two lines of Wallach's poem, which are vague and incomprehensible. A sentence is cut off in the middle, surprising and confusing the reader: "Always holding up a smoky glass/Just in case the sun." In the myth, the sun is a symbol of ferocious masculinity, as the gods (who required Psyche to bring Aphrodite a golden fleece) run amok and kill with their sharp horns and venomous bites. The open closure of the poem presents two alternative interpretations: either Donna Teresa remains unyielding to the end, using the refracted sunlight as a blade against her enemies, or she is protecting herself from her enemies, who are using the sunlight against her.

Mixing Registers

Wallach uses biblical and talmudic sources interpolated with modern Hebrew in an elaborate manner to create a new and original linguistic embroidery and deconstruct the registers of language in her intertext. The prominence of the metaphor רְבוּצָה בְּיָפִי ("wallowing in beauty"), for example, evokes three semantic biblical fields:

1) רָבַץ is typically associated with the characteristics of wild animals, in the way that they crouch down: כָּרַע רָבַץ כְּאַרְיֵה וּכְלָבִיא מִי יְקִימֶנּוּ ("And he crouched and lay down as a lion and as a lion who shall raise him up") (Gen. 49:9).

2) The root רב"ץ ("crouched") is related to beauty: הִנֵּה אָנֹכִי מַרְבִּיץ בַּפּוּךְ אֲבָנַיִךְ ("I will lay thy stones with fair colours...") (Isaiah 54:11); serenity - וְרָבְצוּ וְאֵין מַחֲרִיד (which shall lie down, and none shall make them afraid) (Isaiah 17:2).

3) רב"ץ is also associated with cursing and sinning: וְרָבְצָה בּוֹ כָּל הָאָלָה ("when he heareth the words of his curse")(Deut. 29:19) or with the metaphor רֹבֵץ ("sin lieth [crouches] at the door") (Genesis 4:7).

It is worth noting that in the Bible the verbs שׁוֹבְבוּ ("captivated my heart") and רָבַץ "crouched" appear together in the same verse in two different instances. The most obvious one in Hebrew would be Psalms 23:2-3, one of the most renowned Psalms: בִּנְאוֹת דֶּשֶׁא יַרְבִּיצֵנִי עַל מֵי מְנֻחוֹת יְנַהֲלֵנִי נַפְשִׁי יְשׁוֹבֵב (The King James version has it: "He makes me lie down in green pastures [...] He restores my soul"). The two verbs also appear together in a less known chapter: Jeremiah 50:6: צֹאן אֹבְדוֹת הָיוּ עַמִּי רֹעֵיהֶם הִתְעוּם הָרִים שׁוֹבְבִים מֵהַר אֶל גִּבְעָה הָלָכוּ שָׁכְחוּ רִבְצָם. (The King James version of Jeremiah incorporates the adjective into the noun and translates: "Their shepherds have caused them to go astray, they have turned them away on the mountains [...], they have forgotten their resting place.")

The archaic suffix ־ַתְהוּ, previously mentioned, is used to mark the position of the object before the subject and is incorporated into the predicate, as in the following phrases: בֵּיתָה יִסָּדַתְהוּ בִּבְדֹלַח (literally "Her house she established [it] in crystal") and וְסַכִּינָה בְּפוֹסְפוֹר מְשָׁחַתְהוּ (literally "Her knife with phosphorus she anointed [it]").

Together with its biblical elements, the poem also borrows linguistically from postbiblical strata: words such as קָלַגַּסִים and מְשִׁיחָה in the context of binding are taken from BT Baba Metzia 1:8 כָּל שָׁחוּט אוֹ מְשִׁיחָה אוֹ דָבָר אַחֵר כָּרוּךְ עָלָיו ("anything that has a string or cord tied around it"). The reference to קְלַגְּסִים may subtly allude to an historic event, when a force of legionaries was dispensed to destroy the convents Teresa had founded, which were not tolerated by the male establishment of her day. In the poem the ambiguity of the word מְשִׁיחָה is deftly exploited. On the one hand, the ritual act of installing either a king or the high priest by anointment is evoked, as well as the consecration of certain ritual objects. These undertones surface in the poem's reference to the dagger Donna Teresa has anointed. Here, once more, we can observe a subtle deconstruction of a venerated ritual practice, since Donna Teresa pours oil over the feet of her birds—and the woman-poet elevates the art of falconry above the installation of kings and priests. On the other hand, however, the term מְשִׁיחָה also implies a string used for wrapping—חוּט מְשִׁיחָה. Interpreted in this way, Wallach's character cruelly binds the feet of the birds with string, limiting their freedom. Symbolically, this act may echo the power of a Church that attempts to inhibit the free spirit of women through manipulation and control. Characteristic of Wallach's poetic universe, this ambivalent act is at once both a violent and a polemic gesture.

Wallach does not stop at the deconstruction of her intertext; she also deconstructs registers of language. The nouns, used in their plural form, in conjunction with the subjective genitive, are changed to the grammatical female gender. The feminine ending ה־ (equivalent to ת־) is dominant in mishnaic Hebrew. Such usage creates a unique poetic language, neither biblical nor talmudic, nor identical with any of the preceding linguistic layers. Thus, her bold and original linguistic combinations create a magical and exotic poetic diction.

* * *

Wallach's attitude towards Donna Teresa herself is not agonistic. Through auto-eroticism, assertiveness, and above all, her synthesizing of the sexual and the sacred, Theresa bears more than a passing resemblance to Wallach's other female characters. She is extolled as a woman of action, a woman who successfully challenges the male world, and, through self-assertion, she is shown to empower her own sex.

Moreover, an intertextual reading reminds us that it was often women with intellectual aspirations who entered the convent. Here they could undertake and perform masculine roles through reading and writing about important subjects.

Wallach subverts ideological and cultural norms by intertextual practices and deconstructs the traditional patriarchal code through a new feminist reading of 'אֵשֶׁת־חַיִל' What appears initially to be the laudatory tone of the biblical poem is reevaluated from a feminist perspective. After all, isn't the woman of valor totally dominated by the patriarchal order? The dictum she fulfills is determined by male society: וַתִּתֵּן טֶרֶף לְבֵיתָהּ וְחֹק לְנַעֲרֹתֶיהָ (literally, "She gives portions/rations to her handmaidens.") On a feminist reading, the signifier חֹק means both "portions" and "law": hence, she forces the spirit of the Law of the Father upon her handmaidens. She creates the freedom for her husband to become "famous" and participate in debates with the elders: נוֹדָע בַּשְּׁעָרִים בַּעְלָהּ בְּשִׁבְתּוֹ עִם זִקְנֵי אָרֶץ. He is thus enabled to develop his intellectual skills, while she takes care of the economic needs of the family. There is a disproportionate division of labor between the man and herself. Metaphorically, she is compared to a huntress setting out to track food under cover of dark; and presumably she remains in the darkness of anonymity, since no intellectual qualities are attributed to her. As previously mentioned, even the standards of beauty by which she is approvingly assessed are downgraded at the end of the biblical text.

The semiotic chain is endless. The irony surfacing in Proverbs bounces back and changes in turn the meaning of Wallach's poem. But here a surprising interpretive possibility suggests itself with regard to another canvas on which the poem is overlaid. What, after all, was Donna Teresa's great achievement? In reality, beyond the world of the poem, Donna Teresa set about building convents, which were in fact the ultimate locus of female sexual oppression. In terms of her behavior and sexuality, not only did she choose to live in an autoerotic world, but she also inspired generations of sisters to emulate her. Wallach, the modern woman poet, shatters one stereotype of femininity, but does not suggest another to replace it. Instead she creates a multiplicity of identities and reserves for herself the possibility of entering several embodiments, as well as transmuting herself from these into others.

Wallach's poem responds to the irony of Bernini's work, highlighting the strongly erotic elements that both complement the mystical experience and stand in stark contrast to the proclaimed ideology of the Christian theologians. The angel looks much like Amor, and Donna Teresa is surely overwhelmed by a sensual rather than a spiritual experience. Such irony sheds a helpful light on the deciphering of other intertexts.

In order to explore her own modern identity, Wallach juxtaposes two idealized types of women from different canonic cultural traditions: the "mystic" in Christianity, and "the pious observant" in Judaism. Moreover, in order to wrestle with the Bible, she avails herself of another tradition and a different notion of femininity. The ideal for women in the Jewish tradition was to bear children. The ideal for women in the Christian mystical tradition was marriage with God. By importing Christian myth, Wallach highlights its relevance to her own modern identity, while extracting the archetypes of housewife and huntress in the biblical text.[25] It is in the nature of intertextual encounters that they throw new light on the earlier, as well as on the modern text. As Borges once remarked, in the intertextual process time flies backwards. Wallach's poetry jolts the comfortable scriptural text from its safe niche and opens it up to new readings.

Wallach's poetry is concerned with flux and mutability in time and in language; and Hebrew, within its paradoxical old-new nature, serves her idiosyncratic universe wonderfully. The stylistic violence that is wrought on the language of the patriarchs leads to the marriage of aestheticism and violence and a modern mystical experience.

Hebrew allows the woman poet to write her feminine narrative, not only through structural changes with quotations and references, but also by undermining the words themselves and exploiting their grammatical gender. Moreover, since the Hebrew language exists in a continuum from biblical times, the Israeli poet, as if in a time capsule, can activate the immediacy, accessibility, resonance, and ease of association created by the linguistic layers that are vibrant and preserved in the everyday language of the Israeli reader. As I have argued, Hebrew touches upon archetypes through the spoken language itself, even when the intertext is dormant. The power of Wallach's poetry, like that of many of her contemporaries, stems in part from the effort to secularize the ritualistic element of Hebrew.

Yona Wallach is a Promethean of Language. Her poems deconstruct the word, the sentence, the syntax, the grammar. This deconstruction of language is paralleled with a deconstruction of the "I," which simultaneously enables her to construct various identities. The interaction between text and intertext changes both texts—myth as much as poem. In this way, she establishes a new female identity and a new language for all speakers. She absorbs and incorporates literary and cultural texts organically, to such an extent that one may need to redefine the concept of intertextuality. Her poetry epitomizes the historical process of the appropriation of canonical texts by the contemporary female voice in Israel.

The extent of Yona Wallach's influence can be measured, perhaps, by the fact that she simultaneously won critical recognition and acclaim from the literary establishment and from representatives of "popular culture." But her legacy lies elsewhere, mainly in her daring to take risks. As she shattered the molds, dictums, and taboos of linguistic codes and ideology, she bequeathed the freedom to succeeding generations of artists—women and men—to explore their creativity and to experiment with it.

Concluding Remarks

The Hebrew poet has a noisy existence; when listening for a word he is often prey to echoes—echoes of remote narratives that cling to the word and are often loud and persistent enough to obscure if not drown out its immediate, everyday, serviceable meanings. In such a space the private meaning may be exalted or rendered absurd, and the writer must choose whether to contend with the noise or to try to shut the door on it altogether.

Despite the vivid presence of many historical strata in modern day Hebrew, the Bible remains the principal source of such disruptions. Among other things, it seems to have fixed Hebrew in an obstinate religious mode; semantic presuppositions, idioms and imagery, all containing religious outlooks, force themselves on the secular poet and place obstacles in the way of the evolving vernacular. Paradoxically, however, the very processes of deconstruction and ironization that poets use to secularize their language often serve to revive the original scriptural energy.

In many ways, therefore, modern secular Israeli poetry testifies to the enduring relevance of the Bible. And it is equally true to say that the ongoing duel with the Bible is largely the medium through which Hebrew poetry throughout history enacts its processes of maturation, development, and change.

Notes

The Prophet's Tongue in Our Cheek

1. A.B. Yehoshua, "Eradicating the Aqedah through its Actualization," in *In the Opposite Direction: Articles on Mr. Mani by A.B. Yehoshua*, ed. and intro. Nitza Ben-Dov (Tel-Aviv: Hakibbutz Hameuchad, 1995), p. 396.

2. Ibid. p. 398.

3. Harold A. Bloom, *A Map of Misreading* (Oxford: Oxford University Press, 1975), p. 9.

4. Ibid. p. 10.

5. David Stern, *Midrash and Theory* (Evanston: Northwestern University Press, 1996), p. 37.

6. Ra'aya Harnik, שירים לגוני (Tel Aviv: Hakibbutz Hameuchad, 1983), p. 9.

7. Jonathan Culler, "Presupposition and Intertextuality," in *The Pursuit of Signs: Semiotics, Literature, Deconstruction* (Ithaca: Cornell University Press, 1981), p. 100-119. Culler suggests that linguistic models of presupposition be linked with intertextuality: "Presuppositions are what must be true in order that a proposition be either true or false." [p. 11] "Rhetorically, pragmatically, literally, negations are much richer in presupposition." [p. 115]

8. Ross Chambers, "Alter Ego: Intertextuality, Irony and the Politics of Reading," in *Intertextuality: Theories and Practices*, ed. Michael Warton and Judith Still (Manchester: Manchester University Press, 1990), p. 143.

9. "An intertext is one or more texts which the reader must know in order to understand a work of literature in terms of its overall significance." Michael Riffaterre, "Compulsory Reader Response: The Intertextual Drive," in Warton and Still, op.cit. p. 56.

10. Edward W. Said, *The World, the Text, and the Critic* (Cambridge: Harvard University Press, 1983), pp. 31-53.

11. Natan Zach, *The Penguin Book of Hebrew Verse*, ed. and trans. T. Carmi (Harmondsworth: Penguin, 1981), p. 576.

12. For an extensive study of puns see the anthology *On Puns, the Foundation of Letters*, ed. Jonathan Culler (N.Y.: Basil Blackwell, 1998).

13. *Rhetorica ad Herenniom* IV.xxi: 29, quoted by Culler, op.cit., p. 5.

14. On the function of roots in the reading process, see Ram Frost and Shlomo Benitz, "Reading Consonants and Guessing Vowels: Visual Word Recognition in Hebrew Orthography," in *Advances in Psychology* 94 (1992): 27-44. They write:

> Productive roots have a special status for the Hebrew speaker and reader. Their psychological reality is reflected by their salience relative to the other letters and phonemes constituting the word. It appears that the presentation of a pointed word containing a productive root results in the automatic detection of this root, such that the letters of a word are passed into letters belonging to the root and letters not belonging to it...The phonemes belonging to the root have a unique psychological reality. [p.41]

15. Julia Kristeva, *Séméiotiké : recherches pour une sémanalyse* (Paris, 1969), p. 120.

A Double Bind

1. The Israeli painter Menashe Kadishman, who has dealt almost obsessively with the myth of the binding of Isaac, speaks personally about historical parallels with modern events:

> If I stand on Mount Moriah and look towards the Mount of Olives, I see all this marvelous pink light. There pass before me scenes from the events of the past–love and sacrifice, Abraham and Isaac, David and Absalom, kingdom and fall. The Binding of Isaac occurs in our time, in every place we send our children to wars, but its emblem remains one: Jerusalem–the place where it really happened. [Quoted in Mordechai Omer, *Upon One of the Mountains: Jerusalem in Israeli Art* (The Genia Schreiber Gallery, 1988), p. 127 (bilingual edition).]

2. See Ruth Kartun-Blum, *Préface, Chant D'Israël, Anthologie de la Poésie Hébraïque Moderne*, ed. Nicole Gdalia (Paris: Editions Characters, 1984), pp. 11-50.

3. Shalom Spiegel, *The Last Trial: On the Legends and Lore of the Command to Abraham to Offer Isaac as a Sacrifice: The Aqedah*, trans. with an introduction by Judah Goldin (N.Y.: Pantheon, 1967); (Behrman House, 1979).

4. Erich Auerbach, Mimesis: *The Representation of Reality in Western Literature*, trans. Willard R. Trask (Princeton, NJ: Princeton Univ. Press, 1968).

5. For example, I have excluded the poetry of U.Z. Greenberg, whose engagement with the Aqedah is at odds with that of the majority of the trends discussed here and who deserves a discussion in his own right.

6. Algirdas Julien Greimas, "Les Actants, les actants et les figures," in *Sémiotique narrative et textuelle*, ed. C. Chabzal (Paris: Larousse, 1973). The model I am offering is close to Greimas's actantial one. Greimas distinguishes between "acteur" and "actant." "Actant" refers to general categories in which "acteurs" are invested with specific qualities in different narrations. Greimas maintains that every narrative consists of a restricted set of interdependent roles, although such roles may be played by a very large number of diverse individuals or things. The number of actants is reduced to six in Greimas's model:

Sender → object → receiver
Helper → subject → opponent

See also Shlomith Rimmon-Kenan, *Narrative Fiction: Contemporary Poetics* (London: Methuen, 1983), pp. 29-42. I have used a model of four roles only, but it could easily be expanded into six. The angel, for example–God's voice through a different persona, who averts the sacrifice–might be classified either as a "helper" or an "opponent," depending on our reading of the story. The opponent could also be the Satan of the Talmud (Sanhedrin 18:9b), for God requires proof of resistance to the unsettling voice of Satan, the subjunctive voice of doubt.

7. Shalom Spiegel, *The Last Trial*, p. 69. On the centrality of the idea of transformation, Spiegel says: "If that be the case, then perhaps the whole *Akedah* composition came into being with no purpose other than to teach the lesson and provide the basis for the practice of making a proxy offering." [pp. 68-69]

8. 'על המזבח' ("Upon the Altar"), in כל שירי יצחק למדן, ed. Simon Halkin (Jerusalem: Mosad Bialik, 1982), p. 119. On the theme of the Aqedah in the poetry of Y. Lamdan, see Hillel Weiss, דיוקן הלוֹחם: על גיבורים וגבורה בספרות העברית של העשוֹר האחרון (Portrait of the Warrier: On Heroics and Heroes in Hebrew Literature of the Last Decade) (Ramat Gan: Bar Ilan University Press, 1975), pp. 222-31 (Hebrew).

9. On the confrontation of Hebrew literature with the Zionist master narrative, see Gershon Shaked's seminal essay 'הסיפורת וסיפר העל הציוני' in עצמאות: 50 השנים הראשונות (Independence: The First 50 Years), ed. Anita Shapira (Jerusalem: Merkaz Zalman Shazar, 1998), pp. 487-511.

10. Haim Gouri, שושת רוחות: שירים (Tel-Aviv: Hakibbutz Hameuchad,1960), p 28. Translated by T. Carmi in *The Penguin Book of Hebrew Verse* (London: Penguin, 1981), p. 565.

11. Louis Jacobs, "The Problem of the Aqedah in Jewish Thought," in *Kierkegaard's Fear and Trembling: Critical Appraisals*, ed. Robert L. Perkins (University, AL: Univ. of Alabama Press, 1981), pp. 1-8.

12. Roland Barthes, *Roland Barthes by Roland Barthes*, trans. Richard Howard (NewYork, 1989), p. 145.

13. Translated by Vivian London for this book.

14. In the poetry of the forties and fifties, the narrative of the *Aqedah* is the deep metaphor for the Holocaust. Thus in the 1939 poem by Ezra Zusman, 'ישימו בידך המאכלת' ("They Will Place the Knife in Your Hand"), the lyrical voice warns Isaac: "Push away and block the knife / Isaac, protect yourself." That is also the dominant theme in Uri Zvi Greenberg's רחובות הנהר (The Streets of the River), perhaps the most important Hebrew poetic response to the destruction of European Jewry.

15. On intratextuality as a strategy creating artistic unity in the biblical text, see Robert Alter, "Introduction to the Old Testament," in *The Literary Guide to the Bible*, ed. Robert Alter and Frank Kermode (Cambridge: Harvard University Press, 1987), p. 198.

16. The term is coined by L. Jenny, "The Strategy of Form," in *French Literary Theory Today, A Reader*, ed. Tzvetan Todorov (Cambridge: Cambridge University Press, 1988), pp. 34-36.

17. On the paradigm of the victim becoming redeemer, see Mordechai Shalev's penetrating essay 'חותם העקידה בשלושה ימים מאוחר', מוקדם בקיץ 1970, וּמר מני, in בכיוון הנגדי: קובץ מחקרים על מר מני (In the Opposite Direction, Articles on *Mr. Mani* by A.B. Yehoshua), ed. with an introduction by Nitza Ben Dov (Tel Aviv: Hakibbutz Hameuchad, 1996) (Hebrew). Using Shalev's definition of a "story of destiny," one can categorize Alterman's ballad as a "poem of destiny": "The defining characteristic of a story of destiny is that it is a passage through infinite danger out of which the character marked from childbirth emerges with new strength and readiness for his vocation: the purpose of danger is not only educational, but practical." [p. 413].

18. Yehiel Mar, קווים למעגל (Jerusalem: Kiryat Sefer,1957), p. 50.

19. T. Carmi, שירים. 1951-1969 :דבר אחר (Selected Poems, 1951-1969) (Tel-Aviv: Am Oved, 1974) (Hebrew). 'פחד יצחק' appears in *Selected Poems, T. Carmi and Dan Pagis*, trans. Stephen Mitchell (London: Harmondsworth, 1976), p. 14.

20. Tuvia Rübner, שירים למצוא עת (Tel-Aviv: 1960), p. 105.

21. Auerbach, *Mimesis,* p. 11.

22. David Avidan, 1964–1952 שירים מבחר :מישהו בשביל משהו (Jerusalem: Schocken, 1964), trans. Vivian London.

23. Søren Kierkegaard,*Fear and Trembling*(1843), trans. Walter Lowrie (N.Y.: 1954).

24. Spiegel, *The Last Trial,* p. 109, where he quotes a statement by Resh Lakish in B. Baba Batra 16a: "He is Satan. He is the evil impulse and he is the angel of death."

25. Zalman Schneor, 'עקידות' in שירים, vol. 1, p. 294. (Tel Aviv: Am Oved, 1951).

26. In Benjamin Galai, צפונה מסע (Tel-Aviv: Hakibbutz Hameuchad,1968), p. 46. Translation here by Ruth Kartun-Blum.

27. Indeed, their use of language disproves the contention that the1948 generation wanted to start over from scratch. See Benjamin Harshav, אלפיים, 'מסה על תחיית הלשון' 2(1990): 9-54.

28. In בזכות הנורמליות (Tel-Aviv: 1984,) [*Between Right and Right* (N.Y.: Doubleday, 1981)] pp. 55-59, A.B. Yehoshua offers an interesting psychoanalytical insight into the dominance of the father (God) over the figure of the mother in Jewish consciousness.

29. The accepted meaning of the word שני in this phrase is the same as שנות (years of her life), but through a play on words here, it can be read as two.

30. *Yehuda Amichai, A Life of Poetry, 1948-1994,* selected and translated by Benjamin and Barbara Harshav (N.Y.: Harper-Collins, 1994), p. 345.

31. Benjamin Harshav, "On the Beginnings of Israeli Poetry and Yehuda Amichai's Quatrains," in *The Jerusalem Review,* ed. Gabriel Moked, 1997, p. 18.

32. In the protrayal of the ram, Amichai intuitively echoes a recurrent element in different myths: the sacrificial animals were always those most prized for their human nature.

> The gentlest, most innocent creatures, whose habits and instincts brought them most closely into harmony with man…. From the animal realm those chosen as victims were those which seemed, if we might use the phrase, the most human in nature. [Joseph de Maistre, "Eclaircissement sur les sacrifices," *Les Soirées de Saint-Pétersburg* (Lyons, 1890), quoted by René Girard in *Violence and the Sacred,* trans. Patrick Gregory (Baltimore and London: Johns Hopkins University Press, 1977), pp. 2-3.]

33. In David Avidan, עקרוניים שירים (Axiological Poems) (Jerusalem: Ah'shav, 1978), p. 46. (Hebrew). The translation here is by the poet. See David Avidan, *Cryptograms from a Telestar: Poems, Transmissions, Documents* (Tel-Aviv: 1980), p. 26.

34. *Yitzhak* appears in Amir Gilboa, בבוקר בבוקר שירים ("Songs in Early Morning") (Tel Aviv: Hakibbutz Hameuchad, 1953). The translation here, by T. Carmi, appears in *The Penguin Book of Hebrew Verse,* p. 560. See also the interpretations of the poem by Arieh Sacks in *The Modern Hebrew Poem Itself,* ed. Stanley Burnshaw, T. Carmi, and Ezra Spicehandler (N.Y.: Holt, Rinehart, and Winston, 1965), pp. 136-38, and by Warren Bargad in *To Write the Lips of Sleepers* (Cincinnati: Hebrew Union College Press, 1994), pp. 138-39.

35. See Ram Frost and Shlomo Benitz, "Reading Consonants and Guessing Vowels: Visual Word Recognition in Hebrew Orthography," *Advances in Psychology* 94 (1992): 27-44.

36. Another paronomasia may emerge between the words עלים ("leaves") and עולה ("sacrifice"). Both appear in the biblical narrative and function here as a "siren signifier."

37. Girard (in *Violence and The Sacred*) argues that violence is at the heart of the sacred and of the sacrificial act in myth and ritual, both in the Bible and in Greek tragedy.

38. From Hanoch Levin, מה איכפת לציפור (Tel-Aviv: Hakkibutz Hameuchad,1987), p. 92. The translation here is by Ruth Kartun-Blum

39. The blaming of the fathers brings to mind Wilfred Owen's protest poem from the First World War, *The Parable of the Old Man and the Young:*

So Abram rose, and clave the wood, and went,
And took the fire with him, and a knife
And as they sojourned both of them together
Isaac the first born spake and said, My father
Behold the preparations, fire and iron
But where the lamb for this burnt-offering?
[...]
Then Abram bound the youth with belts and straps
When lo! an angel called him out of heaven
Saying, lay not thy hand upon the lad,
[...]
But the old man would not so, but slew his son
And half the seed of Europe one by one.

The poem is quoted by Benjamin Britten in the *Offertorium* of his *War Requiem*, op. 66.

40. שדמות 35 (1970):19.

41. Avraham Shapira, ed., שיח לוחמים (Tel Aviv: 1967); *The Seventh Day: Soldiers' Talk About The Six-Day War* (London: Deutsch, 1970).

42. Avot Yeshurun, 'השיר על האפריקים ("The Poem on the Africans"), in *The Syrian-African Rift and Other Poems,* parallel text edition, trans. Harold Schimmel (Philadelphia: Jewish Publication Society, 1980), p. 33.

43. Avot Yeshurun, השבר הסורי–אפריקני (Tel-Aviv: Sifrey Siman Kri'a, 1974), p. 11.

44. Avot Yeshurun, ראם (Tel-Aviv: 1961), pp.119-30.

45. Yitzhak Lamdan, כל שירי יצחק למדן, p. 55.

46. S. Yizhar, ימי ציקלג (The Days of Ziklag) (Tel-Aviv: Am Oved, 1958), vol. 2, p. 804 (Hebrew).

47. Mordechai Rotenberg, *Re-Biographing and Deviance: Psychotherapeutic Narrativism and the Midrash* (New York: Praeger, 1987), pp. 104-5.

48. Ibid. p. 108.

49. See David Shulman, *The Hungry God: Hindu Tales of Filicide and Devotion* (Chicago and London: University of Chicago Press, 1993), p. 139.

50. On Ramban's methods for interpreting of the Scriptures, see Amos Funkenstein, סגנונות בפרשנות המקרא בימי הביניים (Styles in Medieval Biblical Exegesis: An Introduction) (Universita Meshuderet, 1990) (Hebrew).

A Modern Mystical Experience

1. Dan Miron, אמהות מייסדות, אחיות חורגות: על שתי התחלות בשירה הארץ־ישראלית המודרנית (Founding Mothers, Step Sisters: The Emergence of the First Hebrew Poetesses and Other Essays) (Tel Aviv, Hakibbutz Hameuchad, 1992) (Hebrew).

2. Wallach's works include the following:

דברים (Poems)(Jerusalem: Ahshav, 1966).

שני גנים (Two Gardens) (Tel-Aviv: Dagah, 1969).

שירה (Collected Poems) (Tel-Aviv: Tel Aviv University Press, 1976).

מופע (Appearance Poems) (Tel-Aviv: Hakibbutz Hameuchad, 1985).

צורות (Forms Poems) (Tel-Aviv: Hakibbutz Hameuchad, 1985).

אור פרא (Wild Light) (Jerusalem: Hakibbutz Hameuchad, rev.ed. 1990).

תדההכרה נפתחת כמו מניפה (Collected Poems 1963-1985)(Tel-Aviv: Hakibbutz Hameuchad, 1992).

3. *Selected Poems 1963-1985* (Tel-Aviv: Hakibbutz Hameuchad, 1992, p. 160.

4. Yigal Sarnah, יונה וולך. ביוגרפיה (Biography) (Jerusalem: Keter, 1992) (Hebrew).

5. Lily Rattok, מלאך האש: על שירת יונה וולך (Angel of Fire: The Poetry of Yona Wallach) (Tel Aviv: Hakibbutz Hameuchad, 1997) (Hebrew).

6. See Tova Cohen, 'בתוך התרבות ומחוצה לה' (Inside Culture and Outside), in Sadan, פרקים נבחרים בשירת נשים עברית (Selected Chapters in Women's Hebrew Poetry) (Tel Aviv: Tel Aviv University, 1997), pp. 69-110 (Hebrew).

7. Alicia Ostriker, *Stealing The Language* (London: The Women's Press, 1987).

8. Adrienne Rich, *Lies, Secrets and Silence* (London: Virago, 1980).

9. Michael Riffaterre, "Compulsive Reader Response: The Intertextual Drive," in *Intertextuality: Theories and Practices,* ed. Michael Worton and Judith Still (Manchester University Press, 1990), p. 57. For a detailed exposition of a theory of meaning and poeticity that relies heavily on intertextuality as well as the dynamics of the reader's experience of the text, see also *Semiotics of Poetry* (Bloomington: Indiana University Press), 1978.

10. "Ivrit," Selected Poems 1963-1985, p. 180.

11. Translated by Ruth Kartun-Blum in cooperation with Miriam Pedatsur.

12. It could also be translated as "Chronicles." The polysemy of the title signals the link between the biblical register and colloquial Hebrew. Rattok suggests that the name is a homage to the last poem in Dalia Hertz's *Margo,* a book that inspired and influenced the poetry of Yona Wallach. (See *Angel of Fire,* op.cit. p. 43).

13. *The Complete Works of St Teresa of Jesus,* trans. E. Allison Peers (London: Sheed and Ward, 1946; single volume ed., 1978).

14. K. Ramus Gil, "Teresa De Hasos," *Hebrew Encyclopedia* 19: 66-68.

15. On the religiosity of Yona Wallach's poetry, see remarks by Rattok in *Angel of Fire,* p. 43.

16. Quoted in Howard Hibbard, *Bernini* (Harmondsworth, 1990), p. 137.

17. This sculpture was chosen as the cover for Hibbard's book and was also one of the two sculptures chosen to represent Bernini's work in the *Hebrew Encyclopedia.*

18. Umberto Eco, *Semiotics and the Philosophy of Language* (Bloomington: Indiana University Press, 1986), pp. 127-28.

19. W. J. T. Mitchell, *Picture Theory* (London: University of Chicago Press, 1994), p. 152.

20. Ibid. p.156.

21. For a discussion of Mitchell's theory of ekphrastic poetry, see Avner Holtzman, ספרות ואומנות פלסטית (Literature and the Visual Arts) (Musag Series, Tel Aviv: Hakibbutz Hameuchad, 1997) (Hebrew).

22. It also echoes the use of שָׁנִים by the prophet Isaiah to signify שָׁנִי ("scarlet"). Isaiah 1:18: אִם־יִהְיוּ חֲטָאֵיכֶם כַּשָׁנִים כַּשֶׁלֶג יַלְבִּינוּ ("Though your sins be as scarlet, they shall be as white as snow"). The original context evoked is one of sin.

23. The signifier פְּנִינִים in the biblical text is translated variously as "rubies," whereas in the modern Hebrew text it is equated with "pearls."

24. Erich Neumann, *Amor and Psyche, On the Development of the Feminine Element: Commentary on the Tale by Apuleius*, trans. Ralph Manheim (N.Y., Bollingen Series) Pantheon Books, 1956.

25. On Christian myths in Wallach's poetry see Arie Sacks, *The Marriage of Paradise and Hell*, הארץ, November 1, 1985.

The Gustave A. and Mamie W. Efroymson
Memorial Lectures

Haim M. I. Gevaryahu
The Theology and Biblical Scholarship of Yehezkel Kaufmann

Arnaldo Momigliano
Aspects of Judaism from the Hellenic and the Roman Angle

Eliezer Schweid
Jewish Survival in Exile: An Israeli View

Bernard Lewis
The Jews of Islam

George L. Mosse
German Jews beyond Judaism

David Winston
Logos and Mystical Theology in Philo of Alexandria

Arthur Green
Devotion and Commandment:
The Faith of Abraham in the Hasidic Imagination

Peter Gay
A Godless Jew:
Freud, Atheism, and the Making of Psychoanalysis

Louis Jacobs
God, Torah, Israel:
Traditionalism without Fundamentalism

Robert Alter
Tradition and Modernity in Kafka, Benjamin, and Scholem

Saul Friedlander
The Historian and the Final Solution

Meir Sternberg
Hebrews in the Hebrew Bible: Poetics, Culture, History

Jeffrey Stout
The Ethics of Poetry

Ruth Kartun-Blum
Profane Scriptures: Reflections on the
Dialogue with the Bible in Modern Hebrew Poetry